ALSO BY T. D. JAKES

Soar!

Inspired to Soar!

Instinct

Destiny

Reposition Yourself

Maximize the Moment

64 Lessons for a Life without Limits

Making Great Decisions

T. D. Jakes Relationship Bible

Great Investment

Ten Commandments of Working in a Hostile Environment

On the Seventh Day

Not Easily Broken

So You Call Yourself a Man?

Woman, Thou Art Loosed!

He-Motions

Mama Made the Difference

God's Leading Lady

Can You Stand to Be Blessed?

Let It Go

Crushing

God Turns Pressure into Power

T. D. JAKES

LARGE PRINT

FaithWords
Hachette Book Group
1290 Avenue of the Americas, New York, NY 10104
faithwords.com
twitter.com/faithwords

First edition: April 2019

FaithWords is a division of Hachette Book Group, Inc. The FaithWords name and logo are trademarks of Hachette Book Group, Inc.

The publisher is not responsible for websites (or their content) that are not owned by the publisher.

The Hachette Speakers Bureau provides a wide range of authors for speaking events. To find out more, go to www.hachettespeakersbureau.com or call (866) 376-6591.

Library of Congress Control Number: 2019930190

ISBNs: 978-1-4555-9537-2 (hardcover), 978-1-4555-9539-6 (ebook), 978-1-5460-3849-8 (ministry signed edition), 978-1-5460-3850-4 (B&N signed edition), 978-1-5460-3565-7 (international), 978-1-5460-1053-1 (large print)

Printed in the United States of America

LSC-C

10 9 8 7 6 5 4 3 2 1

Contents

Contents

CHAPTER I

When Everything Falls Apart

Only through experience of trial and suffering can the soul be strengthened, ambition inspired, and success achieved.

—Helen Keller

"Daddy, I need to tell you something."

No father wants to hear those words from his teenage daughter in the trembling voice with which my youngest daughter, Sarah, spoke them to me and her mother. Sitting there on our front porch, my wife, Serita, and I locked eyes on our youngest child and held our breath in anticipation of the disclosure she was about to reveal. Time stood still as evening unfurled its shadows across the shoulders of the Texas sky and a light breeze wafted the scent of honeysuckle. I knew my daughter was about to reveal something of enormous magnitude.

"I—I'm pregnant!"

The tears she had been fighting to hold back burst the dam of emotion as our baby girl leaned in to wrap her arms around us. As her sobs subsided, Sarah proceeded to share with us the events surrounding her condition, a secret she had been hiding for several months. The strength in her soul exceeded her thirteen years as she summoned every fiber in her being to reveal the fear, turmoil, and excitement coursing through her young heart. Stunned to say the least, I couldn't believe the courage it took for her to confide something so significant in us.

As Sarah cried in my arms, I felt the full weight of the pain and anguish she carried for those several months before she finally unburdened herself. As a parent, you are called to carry the loads of your children that are too heavy for them, and you even want to carry the lighter ones to ease their interactions with the world and everything life will throw at them. My daughter's tears soaked through my shirt as I stroked her hair. Her crying transferred her worry and pain to me, and I felt the growing relief in her heart as she began to realize she wasn't alone.

Soon words were no longer necessary, and the

three of us sat together, a chorus of cicadas the only sound. Tears flowed from my own eyes, and I found my mind wandering. The love and concern I will always have for my daughter were present in that moment as I absorbed the news that I would soon be a grandfather. Despite the bittersweet joy of such news, however, a stinging pain persisted deep in my shattered heart. For you see, only a few months prior, my mother had passed away as a result of Alzheimer's.

One of the bedrocks of my life had just died, and I was still grieving her. Watching the mind of the woman who raised you, cheered you on, chastised you, and fed you vanish piece by piece is a torment I don't wish on anyone. Other than keeping her as comfortable as possible, there was nothing my brother, sister, or I could do. I felt powerless to help my mother retain even the simplest life skills, such as bathing and dressing, and eventually even swallowing.

The wound in my heart from my mother's passing was still raw as I listened to my daughter's confession. I struggled to find a handle on the moment, let alone the past several months. As if my mother's death were not enough, the enemy of my soul seemed to be taunting me with the inability to shield my own daughter from the ways of the world. Once again, I felt crushed by circumstances I never saw coming.

I know it must sound self-centered, but at the time

I couldn't ignore the battle within me as questions and accusations shot through my mind:

You're a terrible father!

Where is your God now?

You're a pastor shepherding others, but you can't even watch out for your own daughter?

You inspire and encourage so many people, but how are you going to do that now? You couldn't protect your mother, and look at you: failing to safeguard your own daughter!

Did Serita and I miss something? Haven't we tried to be good parents? What should I have done differently?

Everything was falling apart.

Far More Fragile

I know I'm not alone in these caustic contemplations. When the floor beneath you opens up and swallows you into a freefall, you find yourself suddenly submerged in a flood of emotions, thoughts, and questions. In the midst of unexpected pain or inevitable loss, these thoughts assail you as you sink into the emotional quicksand of life's messy places, the muddy pits where everything you once held dear and true is questioned, dissected, and shaken to the core.

Here, your safety zone and all presumed constants

are revealed to be far more fragile than you had realized. This is where you wonder if you will ever be on your feet again, and if so, then how you will summon the strength to move on. This is where your faith is tested, where it's refined and purified.

But such knowledge is little comfort in the midst of the blazing wildfires of life engulfing all you thought you knew and reducing expectations to ashes. Like a deer trying to follow a familiar wooded path in the midst of a forest fire, you begin running in circles, facing dead ends and disturbing detours, uncertain which way to go. Choking on collateral smoke, you're left weary and wasted, calloused and confused, depleted and discouraged, frightened and frozen in place.

Part of the confusion results from the way life's greatest successes often bleed into the blur of your most painful moments. Because even in the moments of your greatest anguish, you often find unexpected blessings alongside and commingled with your losses. This was certainly my experience.

Even in the moments of your greatest anguish, you often find unexpected blessings alongside and commingled with your losses.

Even as I watched my beloved mother waste away, I marveled at the way God continued to bless my ministry, my businesses, and my platform of influence. Leaders from around the globe began inviting me to visit, speak, and preach in venues I had once dreamed about seeing. My books were becoming bestsellers, and movie producers were interested in taking *Woman, Thou Art Loosed!* to the big screen as a feature film. But I would have traded all of it for a cure to restore my mother's mind, body, and spirit from the ravages of such an insidious disease.

And now my daughter was pregnant at thirteen. Critics and haters of me and my ministry would pounce on such news like piranhas. Even as Sarah's health and well-being, and the life of my grandchild growing within her, remained my priority, I knew I would be foolish to ignore others' public responses to our family's private situation. The irony of course was that the one person I would usually have turned to for comfort, wise counsel, and encouragement was no longer with me. I would never have my mother back.

I can't tell you the number of nights I cried silently, staring out the windows of my home into the darkness. I never imagined studying the windowpanes would become my default hobby following my mother's death. But night after night, there I was again, gazing into a dark night that reflected the one in my own soul.

Sarah felt better after sharing her news with us and a few other close family members, but I still worried about her. When I wasn't staring out the windows, I was roaming the hallways of my home and peeking into her room to see if she was still with us. Every so often, there was a fear that gripped my heart and made me believe Sarah couldn't handle the shame and embarrassment the world was throwing her way.

As a result, I worried she might take her life in the middle of the night and that neither Serita nor I would know about it until the next morning. Forgive me for imagining such a worst-case scenario, but when the unthinkable happens, suddenly the darkest fears get unleashed from the chains of reason and kennels of faith.

Such was my season at that time. I felt trapped in my pain. Leveled by circumstances beyond my control. Powerless to protect those I loved the most. Unable to enjoy my life's many blessings.

Crushed.

Seeds and Weeds

With all God was doing in my life, some might say there was no way I should have felt so deflated, discouraged, doubtful, and depressed. They would remind me of Jesus' edict "Physician, heal thyself!" (Luke 4:23) and require me to minister to myself with the same conviction with which I preached from the pulpit. But I am just as human as anyone else, and during the crushing blows of life, I'm equally as susceptible to suffering.

More important, I've discovered that if I have anything worth sharing from the pulpit, from the podium, from the boardroom, from movie and television screens, from the pages of the books I write, then it must be authentic to my own experience. I cannot ask you or anyone else to believe in something that I myself haven't tested. If I cannot wrestle with the question of suffering, then I have little to tell you about the sacred.

Is God okay with the coexistence of joy and utter anguish? Do we have to suffer so much loss in this life in order to mature in our faith? Why would a good Father allow his children to suffer so much pain, injustice, and heartache? How can a good God allow anyone to be in a season of life where pain cohabitates with blessing—or worse, to endure a season so bleak that blessings seemed obliterated?

I certainly do not presume to have the answers to such weighty questions, but I have learned the value in asking them—and in experiencing growth as a result of such challenging seasons. During these times, I began to understand the deeper meaning of Jesus' parable about the wheat and tares growing up together (Matthew 13:24–30). We plant seeds of faith that produce a fruitful harvest even as we discover weeds of destructive doubts attempting to destroy our productivity.

Amazingly enough, however, what if our God is so powerful, so good, and so loving that He turns the tables on the tares and uses them to make us stronger, truer, and more dependent on Him? As Joseph explained to the same brothers who had once sold him into slavery and reported him dead to their father, "You intended to harm me, but God intended it for good to accomplish what is now being done, the saving of many lives" (Genesis 50:20). The apostle Paul offers a similar purposeful explanation of pain, "And we know that in all things God works for the good of those who love Him, who have been called according to His purpose" (Romans 8:28).

Amazingly enough, however, what if our God is so powerful, so good, and so loving that He turns the tables on the tares and uses them to make us stronger, truer, and more dependent on Him?

9

Notice that he says *all* things—not some things, a few things, or the good things. *All* includes the hard, the painful, the unexpected, and the seemingly unbearable, unimaginable, and intolerable. *All* includes the losses that you're grieving right now, the ones you carry around inside you every day. *All* includes the disasters, divisions, and distractions intruding on your peace of mind. *All* includes circumstances that leave you feeling powerless, vulnerable, and unsteady on your feet.

In all things God works for the good of those who love Him.

The Master's Marathon

Perhaps you've heard these verses before. You might even be sick of hearing them. Maybe they've been recited rather glibly by well-intended friends or fellow church members in the midst of your life's greatest losses. I'm sure I've even uttered them myself at moments that in hindsight seem poorly timed or unintentionally oblivious to the pain of the soul before me. So allow me to apologize if I've ever led you to believe that the bishop, pastor, speaker, teacher, entrepreneur, movie producer, and author before you has enough faith to somehow avoid encountering the darkest places of life.

In fact, it's just the opposite. I cannot tell you how many times the greatest successes of my life have partnered in tandem with painful ordeals beyond my wildest imagining. From some of my life's greatest hardships, I've discovered my most potent preaching and most meaningful messages. One can't exist without the other if I am to reach the full potential for who God created me to be.

The same is true for you. On one hand, God's purpose is requiring you to step boldly into your future. On the other hand sits the crushing of the accomplishments of your life that you worked and toiled tirelessly to produce. It is the play between these two that compels me to have this conversation with you.

Is it possible—a prerequisite, even—that each person who dares embrace their future is also called to endure a season of trial and pain?

What if there is more to our sufferings than what we see?

What if the disquieting and dreadful places of life often move us along from one stage to the next, a catalyst for our growth unlike any other?

Now more than ever it's crucial that we begin seeing that the plans we have imagined for our lives cannot compare to God's strategy for fulfilling our divine purpose. Once accepted and acted upon, this line of thinking causes a massive shift in our perceptions, decisions, and behavior. We finally realize that we have been thinking on too small a level in contrast to a God whose endgame for our destinies focuses on eternity instead of something temporary. We sprint to win the race we perceive we're running, but instead God is training us for the Master's marathon!

Now more than ever it's crucial that we begin seeing that the plans we have imagined for our lives cannot compare to God's strategy for fulfilling our divine purpose.

Crushing Becomes Creation

I've noticed again and again that routes to progress and success often take detours. Never is there a straight path toward either of them. Our advancement inevitably includes out-of-the-way breakdowns and unplanned pit stops that seemingly have nothing to do with our plans and purpose. We steadily travel down life's highway toward our future until we find ourselves taking an exit to a place that wasn't even on our map. It's an unscheduled stop and perceived pause in our progress that threatens to destroy everything we have accomplished thus far.

Stranded and sidelined, we begin feeling anxious, afraid, and uncertain. As if striking out into something new wasn't jarring enough, we become anxious because we didn't plan on making any stops, let alone in deserted places. But then we discover something there that compels us, inspires us, and motivates us in a new direction. Suddenly we begin blazing a new trail that leads us toward a satisfaction and fulfillment that exceeds anything we could have found using our original itinerary.

And it's all because we got lost along the way to where we thought we were going. Only God knew we weren't lost any more than the people of Israel wandering in the desert for forty years before entering the Promised Land. You see, I'm convinced life's devastating detours often become the miraculous milestones charting a new path toward God's future for us. The tumultuous trying, testing, and crushing we experience in those places is necessary for our advancement. More important, it's imperative that our life's painful detours be hidden from us, lest we forfeit the entire trip toward our future because of our discomfort with being diverted.

In the moment, these crushing places feel like they will destroy us and derail our journey from what we've determined is our destination. We question whether the suffering we're encountering will be the end of all we've accomplished and pursued thus far. We wonder where God is and why He would allow us to hurt so deeply.

But these crushing places also reveal there's more to our lives than what we had planned. They force us to reset our compass on our Creator. As we look for His guidance and follow His direction, the truly invaluable, marvelous, and eternal aspects of our identity and ultimate destiny are then displayed. The crushing becomes the creation of something new. Consider the way tons of rock and soil crush carbon deposits into diamonds. From the carbon's perspective, the weight of the world literally destroys you—but it also creates something new, something rare and beautiful.

There's another analogy that I find even more compelling, one that permeates the Bible in both the Old and New Testaments, and that's the process of winemaking. Addressing an agrarian culture, many of the images, metaphors, and parables of Scripture focus on planting, tending, gardening, and harvesting. The journey from seed to sapling, from grape to greatness, consistently remind us of the process. These symbols lend themselves to our spiritual growth and development as well.

When we first step into an area where we are able to grow, is that not analogous to us being planted? Later, when we encounter a blessing in our lives, can it not be seen as fruit to be enjoyed? When our family and friends revel in our success, is that not akin to those farmers of old relishing the harvest?

When our harvest doesn't go as planned, however, and our fruitful blessing is stripped from us and carelessly trampled, does that not strongly resemble the winepress, the device used to crush grapes and drain their juice for winemaking?

Of course, all of this depends on your point of view. If you were a winemaker, or vintner as they're often called, you would be all too familiar with each step in the process of making wine. However, if you were the grapevine, the removal of your fruit and its destruction under the feet of those who seem not to care would give you a completely different perspective.

In the midst of our painful crushing, we realize that the blessing found in the production of fruit in our lives was never God's end goal. Our latest crop of fruit was merely part of an ongoing, greater process. The Master Vintner knows there's something much more worthwhile beyond the production of fruit— the potency of its juice fermented into wine. To the vine, however, the fruit seems to be everything, season after season, storm after storm, sun and rain, spring and fall. But what if you shifted your paradigm to winemaking instead of fruit growing?

Our latest crop of fruit was merely part of an ongoing, greater process.

Could it be possible that your current predicament is the winepress God uses to transform your grapes into His wine? Could being crushed be a necessary part of the process to fulfill God's plan for your life? Could you be on the verge of victory despite walking through the valley of broken vines?

A Vintage Transformation

On one hand, God's purpose is requiring you to step boldly into your future. On the other hand sits the crushing of the accomplishments of your life that you worked and toiled tirelessly to produce. It is the play between these two that compels me to have this conversation with you. Just like my daughter in that fateful revelation of her unplanned pregnancy, is it possible—a prerequisite, even—that each person who dares embrace their future is also called to endure a season of trial and pain?

What if there is truly more to our sufferings than what we see? If you're anything like me, maybe you have discovered the disquieting and dreadful places of crushing in life move us along from one stage to the next. We may not like to admit it, but what if our crushing is necessary in order for our potential to be fulfilled?

No matter our season of life, I believe it is crucial to our development that we begin seeing that the plans we have imagined for our lives do not even compare with the Master's strategy. Once accepted, this line of thinking causes a massive shift in our perceptions. We finally realize that we have been thinking on too small a level in contrast to a God, whose endgame for our destinies resembles eternity instead of something temporary.

Can you see the necessity of being crushed as part of your maturation process to fulfill God's plan?

Crushing places reveal that there is more to our lives than we had planned. The truly invaluable, marvelous, and eternal aspects of our identity and ultimate destiny are displayed to us there. It is in the midst of painful crushing that we realize that the blessing found in the production of fruit in our lives was never the Master's end goal. Our latest crop of fruit was merely part of an ongoing, greater process.

It is specifically upon the areas of personal crushing that I want us to focus our exploration in these pages. We don't need to linger on what the moments of crushing actually feel like, because every person of destiny has or will become familiar with pain. The question that needs to be answered during our crushing is whether or not the suffering we are encountering is the end of all we have accomplished. To that inquiry, I sincerely and wholeheartedly believe the answer is a resounding "No!"

The question that needs to be answered during our crushing is whether or not the suffering we are encountering is the end of all we have accomplished. To that inquiry, I sincerely and wholeheartedly believe the answer is a resounding "No!"

The process of making wine takes time. And it's not just the actual process of picking the grapes, sorting out the ripe fruit from that which is not ready or has spoiled, crushing the fruit, and letting it ferment into alcohol as the juice becomes wine. Even after the wine has been bottled, it may be years before it is at its peak and ready to be served. Have you ever noticed the way fine wines may be decades old? A wine aficionado would know not only the vineyard, its geographical region and climate, and the specifics of the type of wine—chardonnay or merlot, for example, but they would also know the vintage and the quality of wine produced that year.

From the grape's point of view, that year in which they were picked and crushed seemed devastating at the time, but for the vintner and later the fortunate few sipping the delicious bottle of wine from that vintage, the year now seems like a blessed time, a time of transformation.

That's what this book is about: *your transformation*. Could the worst moments of your life actually become turning points of triumph for God, the Master Vintner, as He uses your life's deepest heartaches and most devastating disappointments for your good and His glory?

When my precious daughter, barely more than a child herself, told me she was carrying a child of her own, I thought I would die. But when I look at her now, and the incredible ministry she shares with her husband, I know that she would not be where she is without the crushing she endured. When I look at the young man my grandson has become, I know that what seemed like a crushing disclosure at the time has fermented into a trophy vintage of our Father's best wine.

Perhaps you have already witnessed such fermentation in your own life and are grappling to understand why God would use such horrific means to produce such undeniable blessings in your life. Maybe you are facing a crisis of faith at this very moment as you wrestle with the bruises of your battered spirit amid the crushing blows of life. It need not even be an event of undeniable magnitude, such as a divorce or layoff at work that leaves you reeling. Sometimes the cumulative impact of our crushing leaves us drained of our ability to see the divine on display in the ruins of our restoration.

You might feel resigned to a life that's less than God's best for you because you cannot allow yourself to imagine that the best is yet to come. Even though the event itself may have been years or decades ago, the trauma of your tragedy may continue to trap you in the past moment, leaving you to focus on the broken stems and crushed fruit of your past achievements rather than the possibility of maximizing your potential through our Father's process of fermentation. Regardless of where you are, we all wrestle with the unexpected impact that crushing leaves on our souls.

Could there be sanctity in your suffering?

Could your worst moments truly become more than shameful secrets of your past mistakes?

What if you could see your life as God sees it?

What if your best moments are waiting ahead?

My friend, I'm convinced God can use the weight crushing your soul right now to create His choicest wine—if you will let Him.

Crushing is not the end!

CHAPTER 2

Quality Control

Always remember, you have within you the strength, the patience, and the passion to reach for the stars to change the world.

—Harriet Tubman

As we all came to terms with Sarah's revelation, I struggled with how to function in the midst of such a feeling of powerlessness. While I believe thoughtful consideration is essential for wise decisions, there was no due diligence I could discern that could change this situation. I had to come to terms with a new reality, one I had not foreseen or could have ever imagined. Losing my mother, and especially in a way that required me to lose her both before and after her last breath, and suddenly feeling like I had lost Sarah to a world intent on taking her from me—I felt buried in grief.

I am not one to wallow in self-pity, but when I experienced that one-two punch to my soul, I could only sink into the quicksand of my sadness. So many nights I stared out the windows of my home, seeing in the darkness nothing but the reflection of my own glistening tears as they coursed down my face. I usually prefer to take constructive action in the midst of any mistake, mishap, or misadventure, but my new reality left me drained of my determination.

Somehow I could not abandon my calling to facilitate faith in the lives of others, but I also could not understand why God had allowed these two soul-numbing events to transpire—and so close to each other in time. I felt like a spiritual navigator who no longer had the personal GPS he had come to rely on. Instead, I had to return to something much more basic and fundamental, a trailblazer once again gazing at the stars for direction.

I was preaching, teaching, and leading others while I struggled to navigate through deep emotions that were grossly uncharted. It was at that stage of my personal development that I found myself being planted. My outer shell was beginning to rot away so that what God placed in my core would begin to flourish.

But I knew this would be a process, one that would try my patience again and again. Even as I knew Sarah must carry her baby nine months in order for it to develop and mature enough to deliver, I struggled to understand how we would all endure the journey from that day on the porch until that moment in the delivery room when the cries of a newborn would punctuate our celebration of his or her arrival.

How could I endure pushing through the cold, dark ground until then?

How long would I have to cry into the darkness?

How would I get through this time?

Hurry Up and Wait

Despite knowing that any new creation requires time, I still struggled in the moment. But as Thanksgiving approached and I began to plan my contribution to the major meal for our family's gathering, I realized that I would rather wait than rush. Because when it comes to the kitchen, I believe anything worth serving is worth waiting for.

You see, anyone who knows me knows that I absolutely love to cook. Whenever I have leisure time I head to the kitchen, and I have a few rules. One is that I don't like to follow recipes, savoring instead the culinary creativity that must motivate master chefs. My other requisite is a group of family and friends to indulge my endeavors—and they must be hungry! A few polite bites is an insult. I love to cook for people who loosen their belts when they're eating and consider their grunts and lack of choice manners to be the greatest compliments—along with asking for seconds and thirds, of course.

My passion for cooking meals for loved ones originated when I was growing up. Because our family didn't have much materially, my siblings and I didn't get excited about gifts at Christmas and birthdays—but we were exuberant in anticipation of the food! I remember my mother preparing and cooking food for days before Christmas. You could smell the aromas wafting throughout the house, and if you were lucky, she would allow you to lick the spoon and taste a little bit beforehand. As a result, my wife and I now delight in showing the same love my mother put into the preparation of special meals into the celebrations we enjoy.

From all those years of watching my mother prepare food for the family, and from my own limited experience in the kitchen, I've realized an important lesson: *quality takes time*. While most people tend to agree with me, no one particularly enjoys waiting patiently for the turkey to come out of the oven or for the pie crust to be made from scratch. We want the quality, but we don't want to wait for it.

Quality takes time.

As I look around, it doesn't take much to see that this current generation is accustomed to fast foods, instant information, and new friendships at the click of a button. Because of such immediate results, we've ignored the diminishing quality of those things we receive instantly and our subsequent lack of appreciation for them. Our desire for instant gratification has ushered us to the point that we sacrifice excellent quality because of the difficulty and time it takes to produce it.

Planting with Patience

Considering the amount of work it takes to produce a great meal reminds me of the way we discover and utilize what God has placed inside us, the core gifts, talents, abilities, and preferences unique to our Creator's design. Throughout our lives and amid the diverse variables of our particular environments, the same God who placed those seeds and gifts within us seeks to cultivate and harvest His initial investment in order to multiply it even more. Our Maker wishes to see these internal seeds and latent talents grow, mature, and bring forth abundant fruit used for something more.

Because God is the originator of everything in us, and because we are created in His image, it makes sense that He desires to see His creativity exercised in His creations. If the cycle of nature calls for us to reproduce after our own kind, we logically see that same inclination in the Creator, who set this cycle into motion. His intention is for the seeds placed inside us to grow, develop, mature, and maximize our growth.

Our current world, however, demands hurriedly produced results, and many of us have despised the day of small beginnings found in seeds. It is a fact that seeds take time to grow. You do not plant a seed today and expect a harvest tomorrow. We often don't exercise the patience to wait and watch and wait some more.

But patience may be the ultimate source of quality control for what God is simmering in your soul and cooking up in your life. The real mystery of God is hidden in the beauty of the seed and revealed in His wonderful use of the growth process. So if we abort the development process, we are compromising the power of the promise God has placed within us. After all, the process of a seed becoming what is promised is the underlying realization of our destiny.

Taking one step in the right direction toward your destiny right now does not equal you seeing your future in all its glory tonight. Who we are, the fruit we are meant to produce, and the wine into which God transforms us requires more—and deserves more—than to be rushed by a microwave mindset that will yield underdeveloped results. Genuine, personalized, noteworthy quality requires the luxury of time. With each of us being high-quality seeds the Master has planted, a half-hearted maturation process would sabotage His plan to transform us into something extraordinary.

Taking one step in the right direction toward your destiny right now does not equal you seeing your future in all its glory tonight.

Packed with Promise

One of the most beautiful depictions of the powerful promise packed in a seed emerges in some of Jesus' last words to His followers before His crucifixion. Meeting in a private upper room, Jesus and His disciples had gathered to celebrate Passover, where he told them:

> I am the true vine, and my Father is the gardener. He cuts off every branch in me that bears no fruit, while every branch that does bear fruit He prunes so that it will be even more fruitful. You are already clean because of the word I have spoken to you. Remain in me, as I also remain in you. No branch can bear fruit by itself; it must remain in the vine. Neither can you bear fruit unless you remain in me. (John 15:1–4)

The symbolic references Jesus assigns to Himself, to God the Father, and to us as His followers demand our attention. The distinctive roles within His overriding metaphor convey key aspects of our personal and spiritual development in ways that His followers would immediately understand. Christ's metaphor speaks to the very nature of who God is, why Christ came, who we are, and what God has been up to since Adam and Eve left the Garden of Eden after disobeying their Creator. A relationship exists between us, the Savior, and the Creator that Jesus plainly sets before us by using this powerful analogy.

Instead of gardener, other translations often render the word referring to God's role as vinedresser, a specific type of farmer responsible for cultivating grapevines. From the vines the Creator cultivates, we can conclude that God desires vines with fruit-bearing branches. Jesus is the vine, and we the branches depend on Him for life. We can do nothing without Christ, who facilitates and sustains the vital growth process between us and our Creator and Cultivator. Jesus is the point of reconnection for us back to God and God to us.

We aren't capable of producing fruit by ourselves. We must be connected, nourished, and strengthened by our Vine even as we serve the purposes of the Vinedresser. The latent potential within us can only be realized under horizontal pressure for vertical purposes.

We must be connected, nourished, and strengthened by our Vine even as we serve the purposes of the Vinedresser.

Designed for Eternity

Consider the biological growth of a human being from conception to full maturity. The sperm, or seed, of an adult male fertilizes and fuses with the ovum, or egg, of an adult female. That fertilized egg develops into an embryo and then a fetus over a nine-month period. At the end of the fetal stage, a baby is born into the world. Over a period of years, the infant grows into a toddler and then advances into childhood, adolescence, and finally adulthood.

Notwithstanding any illnesses or other challenges, not a single child brought into this world ever remains in seed form. Not one of us is a large, fertilized ovum roaming the neighborhood. Each of us became something greater. We grew into the full maturity of our potential.

What we see in the natural realm is a reflection of what we see spiritually, because both are intertwined with each other. As a result, we encounter another version of natural child development in our spiritual nature. In the spiritual realm, there is a process we enter into in which God cultivates and develops us into a healthy vine in His vineyard, and God has made Jesus to be the type of vine we are to exemplify in each stage of life.

For instance, we already know Christ became human so that He would be familiar with each of our trials, difficulties, and temptations. In essence, He experienced all of the growth pains we would experience. As Jesus grew in stature, we know that He grew in favor with God and with men and began bearing fruit. Though He was an adult producing a wonderful harvest during His three years of ministry, He did not come to earth to simply work miracle after miracle. He intended to move from something temporary to something eternal.

Though Christ became a physical adult, His spirit carried within it the even greater promise of an eternal harvest, and not just one made up of miracles that would be temporarily praised. In order for that spiritual promise to be birthed, the supernatural seed had to enter into its own version of development. Like any seed that sprouts, it had to be planted. In essence, everything the seed knows about itself has to end. The seed, then, must die just as Christ died so that He could give birth to us.

Just as He intended with Christ, God never destined us to remain in seed form. He did not design us in such a fashion, because nothing eternal could ever exist temporarily. God's desire has always been to reconnect us back to Himself and take us from finite to infinite. One of the things I love most about

God's Word is how God addresses every season of life: beginning, middle, and end. If Jesus is God's only begotten Son, how could we not assign the same timeless and eternal nature to Him that we view in God? In fact, this truth is the foundation from which John begins his gospel account of the life of Christ:

> In the beginning was the Word, and the Word was with God, and the Word was God. He was with God in the beginning. Through Him all things were made; without Him nothing was made that has been made. In Him was life, and that life was the light of all mankind. The light shines in the darkness, and the darkness has not overcome it . . .
>
> The Word became flesh and made His dwelling among us. We have seen His glory, the glory of the one and only Son, who came from the Father, full of grace and truth. (John 1:1–5, 14)

Since Jesus is the very fruition of God's Word, He must be the beginning, or seed, of our lives as well. The seed, then, was already present because Jesus is simultaneously the vine and seed. Therefore, the seed and vine are one.

Confused? I know it's mind-bending and requires

some reflection. Perhaps the apostle Paul explained it best in His letter to the Galatians: "The promises were spoken to Abraham and to his seed. Scripture does not say 'and to seeds,' meaning many people, but 'and to your seed,' meaning one person, who is Christ" (Gal. 3:16).

With Jesus being the seed promised to Abraham as an inheritance, we must ask ourselves what the promise was inside of Jesus that was to be fulfilled. The promise carried by Christ is a bountiful harvest of fruit. Since Jesus is both seed and vine, we are the promised fruit-bearing branches that spring forth from Him. During the Last Supper, we see the Seed of Abraham speaking with his spiritual offspring that would soon take up the task of not only bearing fruit but also pointing other dormant seeds of promise back to the life-giving Savior, Jesus Christ. If Jesus is the seed that grew into a vine that produced us as fruit-bearing branches, the fruit we produce and lives we live are seeds that God intends for a greater purpose.

If Jesus is the seed that grew into a vine that produced us as fruit-bearing branches, the fruit we produce and lives we live are seeds that God intends for a greater purpose.

We were created to be more than temporary fruit—*we are His eternal wine in the making!*

Dirty Places

How does this process of fermentation into eternal wine occur? Here's the short answer: over time in dirty places. What we see in the natural realm is a reflection of what we see spiritually because both are intertwined with one another. As a result, we encounter another version of natural child-into-adult development in our spiritual nature. In the spiritual realm, there is a process we enter into in which God cultivates and develops us into a healthy vine in His vineyard, and God has made Jesus to be the type of vine we are to exemplify in each stage of life. Jesus is our perfect example, our model of this intended maturation.

For instance, we already know Christ to be the Seed of Abraham. He came in our likeness so that He would be familiar with each of our trials, difficulties, and temptations (Heb. 4:15–16). In essence, He experienced all of the growth pains we would experience. As Jesus grew in stature, we know that He grew in favor with God and with men and began bearing fruit (Luke 2:52). Though He was an adult producing a wonderful harvest during His three years of ministry, Jesus was not meant to simply work miracle after miracle. His life on earth was intended to move from something temporary to something eternal.

Though Christ became a physical adult, His spirit carried the even greater promise of an eternal harvest—and not just one made up of miracles that would be temporarily praised. In order for that spiritual promise to be birthed, the supernatural seed had to enter into its own version of development. Like any seed that would sprout, it had to be planted. In essence, everything the seed knows about itself has to end. The seed, then, must die just as Christ died so that He could give birth to us as God's spiritual children, His divine offspring.

If we are called to be like Christ, to become like Him as we are called by God (1 Cor. 11:1), we must accept the fact that we will experience a similar growth process. As we undergo maturation, we come to understand that our temporary fruit was never the endgame of an everlasting Master, but rather just a single step in the process of making eternal wine. As a result, our spiritual development from seeds to mature fruit-bearing branches demands that we confront a step that many of us grapple with understanding: growing in dirty places.

Our spiritual development from seeds to mature fruit-bearing branches demands that we confront a step that many of us grapple with understanding: growing in dirty places.

When everything falls apart in our lives, we are broken but not destroyed. The exterior husk we've all relied on for so long begins to fail us as the waters of life softens our protective coating. The tender inner life and identity of who we are is naked and helpless in front of those things that threaten the only existence we know. When we are placed in perilous circumstances, we rush to secure ourselves and hold everything in place. We shoot roots into the soil beneath us in hope of anchoring ourselves against life's storms. We yearn for someone or something to hold us, lift us, and sustain us, but too often we droop and wilt in the winds of our isolation and loneliness.

How do you respond to being broken by life? Where do you try to put down roots to secure your life source? Do you focus on acquiring money only to find that it doesn't fulfill you? Do you reach for sex only to discover that the touch of another person is just a reflection of your own aloneness? Perhaps you reach for church only to realize that religion without

God's voice is nothing more than sprinting inside a hamster wheel.

Whatever it is that we do while trying to maintain balance and security, sooner or later we typically feel stuck. Our roots stay in place as we strain for the thing we believe will make it all better, because everyone reaches for something when it seems God is silent. After each failure of ineffective actions we hoped would anesthetize the pain, we stretch ourselves to touch something—anything—that would make our loneliness and discomfort more bearable.

In our rush to escape the pain, messiness, and brokenness of our lives, however, we often miss our opportunities for growth. Mired in the muck of our misguided mindsets, we miss what God may be doing in the midst of this dirty place. With a heave, a strain, a shove, a stretch, and a charge upward, you fight to leave the place you were planted, because surely you believe that God has to have something better for you than where you've come from and where you are.

Your core cries for you to get out of that abusive home. Your heart yearns for escape from poverty. Your gifts expand and surge as you seek to grow your business. "Surely," you say in the midst of God's apparent silence, "He will not abandon me in this place of death."

Right when you've lost all hope, you see something

you have never witnessed before. When you resolved within yourself that maybe, just maybe, where you are is your assigned lot in life, God remains vocally silent but reminds you of His promise by showing you the light you have never seen. You move toward the light, slowly stepping out in faith despite all the pain, filth, shame, and suffering.

Breaking through the dark soil of where you were placed in life, you sprout and rise to continue seeing another world of possibilities. The dirty place became the nurturing soil that enabled you to grow and blossom in ways you would never have experienced sitting in the safety of a greenhouse.

Buried to Blossom

Most people love the thought of being gifted and having the ability to do something great, but we don't smile so brightly when we are placed in the refining processes of life. But what happens to a seed if it's not planted? Jesus said, "Very truly I tell you, unless a kernel of wheat falls to the ground and dies, it remains only a single seed. But if it dies, it produces many seeds" (John 12:24).

We cannot rightfully ask our Vinedresser to skip out on the development of our lives simply because we are uncomfortable with being alone in dark places. To keep a seed from being planted is to condemn that seed to never realize its full potential. It is a fact that seeds are meant to be covered and die.

To keep a seed from being planted is to condemn that seed to never realize its full potential.

No matter who we are, where we are in life, or where we've come from, we must begin to appreciate the ugly stages of our inception. When we allow the Lord to shift our mindset, we begin to see that everything that has ever happened to us has happened for a reason. If we look back at the sprout that pushed itself through the ceiling of dirt above it, we discover reasons behind our adversity that were previously invisible and unimaginable but now are suddenly apparent and miraculous when we arrive at the fruit-bearing stage.

Looking back, I examine previous periods of my life and remember how fearful I was in the midst of some of them. Now standing upon just over forty years of ministry, I look at those places and realize they were integral to where God has taken me and where He will continue to take me. I see that each growth interval of my life was preceded by a planting phase where I was buried in a dirty place. I began to understand that the stages in my life where, at the time, I was certain I was about to meet my end were seed stages for the next season. I could not have produced the fruit without the frustration. And God could not ferment my fruit into His wine for maximum potency without my willingness to relinquish it to His winepress.

Though I have not liked the process, my faith has grown deeper as I discovered this new perspective. I have been changed by this shift in perspective as I accept that God never intended to lead me to a dead place and leave me there. The seeming death through which He escorted me was merely the precipice of a new beginning, and a new beginning is what the planting and death of each seed is all about. Through those stages, I arrived at the truth: *God wasn't burying me—he was planting me.*

Those areas and times in which the death of a dream, assignment, or vision seems to stalk your every move are nothing more than entrances into the next realm of your life. Do not run from them. Embrace them, because the proverbial death of what you are trying to keep alive will enrich the growth and lives of others.

Transformation requires sacrifice, and I wonder if

you have misinterpreted the Vinedresser's intention. Instead of condemning you to a graveyard, which is what you may feel, God is planting you in richer soil for greater fruit.

God is planting you in richer soil for greater fruit.

Humbled by Hindsight

Allowing my mind to drift back to that day with Sarah on the porch, I marvel at what God has done in all our lives. If I could've known then what I know now, I wouldn't have felt so conflicted about her tear-filled announcement to me. To see the woman she is, the family she has, the mother she has become to all her children, and the wife and co-pastor she has become to my son-in-law is nothing short of a perfect example of what God can do when He is allowed to have His way.

To now realize that God had placed her, my then unborn grandson, and me in such symmetrical proximity to one another is mind-blowing. Inside my daughter was the physical manifestation of a seed maturing into something that would soon leave the soil of Sarah's womb. Sarah, at such a young age, was pushed into the dirty soil of who and what she is now. Not only did she have to learn how to be a mother, Sarah was being taken on a crash course in responsible adulthood. Where she had a child in her early teens, she is now sharing with her husband the responsibility of rearing spiritual children that will bear natural and eternal fruit of their own.

Then, there was me. I discovered that Sarah becoming a mother required me to shed old patterns of thought in order to become the father and grandfather she and my grandson would need. I was taken back through spiritual first grade to relearn some fundamentals of faith in a new way. My family had changed. My perspective was altered. The bishop from whom pastors and world leaders sought wisdom was having to stay after school with God to receive tutoring in areas where he had no experience. I was humbled and forced to rely on God and to walk by faith like never before.

Admittedly, how God decided to develop me in the process was quite unorthodox. It was dark. It was ugly. It was dirty. But looking back at it all, I realize that every dirty place of death was so worth the life and fruit that He has produced in my life now.

The same is true for you. God is at work, and there's no place too dirty for Him to use as the rich soil of your maturation and spiritual fruition. Wherever you are, or whatever your dirty place might be, look around you and allow the Master to adjust your thinking. After all, God is not done with you yet.

Quality takes time, and you are God's masterpiece.

CHAPTER 3

The Strategy of Cultivation

As I walked out the door toward that gate that would lead to my freedom, I knew if I didn't leave my bitterness and hatred behind, I'd still be in prison.

—*Nelson Mandela*

Imagine spending your entire day rolling a giant boulder, one you can barely push because of its crushing weight, up to the top of a hill. Then imagine having to roll that rugged rock downhill the next day, back to where you started. Then back up again. Day after day, you labor and strive and sweat to move that rock, only to cover the same hard, rutted ground. No satisfaction, only stagnation.

This punishment emerges not from any cruel conjecture of my own imagination but from ancient mythology and the story of a man named Sisyphus. After committing heinous crimes against the gods, Sisyphus was condemned to spend eternity rolling that rock up and down a mountain. The twentieth-century existential philosopher and author Albert Camus drew on this story for exploring his thoughts on life, meaning, and purpose in a famous essay, "The Myth of Sisyphus," in which he compares our plight to that infamous icon of ancient Rome.

Myths and fables are one thing, but the cold, harsh reality of incarceration is another. I'm grateful that I have never known such punishment. Being stripped of my freedom of choice and deprived of the ability to experience new opportunities and visit exciting places is a horror I don't ever want to encounter. I thrive in change and detest the stagnation of being stuck in endless cycles of futility. And, yet, that's the intention with imprisonment.

No, I can't imagine twenty-seven days in a jail cell, let alone the twenty-seven years endured by Nelson Mandela. The man who would go on to become the president of South Africa suffered wrongful imprisonment for taking a stand against the racial and social injustices of apartheid. Upon hearing such news, today's civil rights leaders and activists would be in an uproar and feverishly fighting for change because each of us, on some level, values the gift of freedom. After all, what good could ever come from imprisoning an innocent man?

Could it be that we ask such questions because we're missing a greater strategy? What if prison was President Mandela's dirty place, the horrific field where everything that made him a great leader was cultivated and refined? When I consider the entire mosaic of President Mandela's life, I find it difficult to ignore the impact that those obviously dreadful twenty-seven years had on him, let alone the lives of his family and loved ones. But looking at the story of his life in whole and not just in that one stretch of almost three decades, it's hard not to see the nurturing impact such suffering seeded. If the Master was working on something extraordinary in President Mandela's cell, we're forced to examine our own lives through the same lens and realize that God had a strategy in the ugly places because those were the fields in which he decided to cultivate us.

God had a strategy in the ugly places because those were the fields in which he decided to cultivate us.

49

Sprouted Seedlings

Have you noticed our human propensity to brood over the disastrous at the expense of the prosperous? We do anything and everything to avoid the hideous experiences of life, never grasping the fact the sprouted seedling could never understand the process of cultivation from its own limited point of view. Similarly, it is a striking blow to our limited comprehension of God to accept that he would use the most unorthodox procedures and inhospitable environments to develop us into something more, something teeming with the potential for dynamic growth. But what's better than being undone and marred in the hands of the Master if a new way of living and abundance are the promised results? What if all you've suffered in your life without was necessary to cultivate your greatness within?

We fight against God's sovereignty because we dislike where His process has placed us. Where the Lord found you, however, and where He decides to plant you can be quite different. We're all being grafted into a supernaturally cultivated vine, and this merging takes time and costs us the comfort of everything we consider comfortable and familiar. Having your life upended and every recognizable detail removed from your environment produces trauma.

But the Master is intentional in how He relocates the wild shoots of our lives and moves them into the unrecognizable fields of promise. This is the secret to accepting the visible violence of turbulent times: we must remember that soil must be upturned or else it will go fallow, depleted of its nutrients and minerals and unable to accommodate new growth.

The act of cultivation is married to our purposeful displacement, because anything grown in the wild does so without the careful hand and watchful eye of an intentional vinedresser. Cultivation speaks order into chaos, orchestrates harmony from disharmony, draws care from carelessness, and provides direction to aimlessness. Cultivation carries within its roots the desire to grow and create where and in a manner that growth and creation are impossible.

Any farmer or agriculturist understands this, but many of us miss the point within our own lives. We choose our own way of seeing, believing, and acting because we think we know better. As a result, we miss our true identity and the blessings we could have had if we would have simply submitted to the process.

God is adamantly invested in developing us into something we would never be without His direct intervention. When we find ourselves broken, battered, beaten, and bruised by our circumstances, it's possible that the Master who we're praying will remove and solve the problem is the very One who sanctioned it and is using it to accomplish some greater effect.

God is adamantly invested in developing us into something we would never be without his direct intervention.

Stumbling in Cultivation

Out of all my years of teaching, preaching, mentoring, and living through hellish ordeals, I believe that our maturation requires that we be constricted to His methods and imprisoned by His purpose. You see, I've had the privilege of meeting some of the most interesting people in the world—and no one was more surprised than I was! In my wildest dreams, I never imagined sitting across from the CEO of AT&T or getting to see Oprah Winfrey move and operate in the worlds of film, television, and print media because the seed of who I was could not comprehend the fruit I would bear and the wine I would become.

I didn't suddenly wake up as the person you see today. I was developed into this, and God is still fostering even more within me. None of what you see in my life today happened because of magic, luck, or happenstance. All of it is the fruit of purpose, cultivation, and time—the culmination of myriad random details coalescing into something beautiful.

Let me illustrate what I mean. My wife, Serita, and I never had any desire to do films. We started off preaching and doing gospel plays and nearly lost everything in our attempts to get them off the ground. Finally, we figured out how to be semi-successful with them and took the stage version of *Woman, Thou Art Loosed* to Atlanta. There, we happened to bump into Tyler Perry, but not the Tyler Perry you know of today. Each of us were seeds in the field of entertainment, and none of us really understood the power of what we were doing. We were just stumbling around, trying to survive while we ministered the gospel in a unique way.

WTAL eventually made it to Los Angeles, and there we met Reuben Cannon, a film producer who helped introduce us to Hollywood. This was a project that my wife and I believed would make it no further than the stage, let alone to select television screens. All the while, it seemed as if we were haphazardly moving from one blessing—one moment—to the next. It was in the fields of preaching and entertainment that Serita and I finally gained the slightest understanding that what the Lord had planned for us was far bigger, better, and brighter than what we had in mind. But, that fruit wouldn't suddenly appear. The Vinedresser would take us through a uniquely constructed process of cultivation that would lead to the development of the fruit you see today.

Much like we did, you might find yourself stumbling from one season of your life to the next, wondering about the answer that would help you connect the dots that often seem so chaotic and disconnected. Having been displaced, dislocated, and dislodged from the comfortable environment you believed was best for you, you now find yourself stumbling around in circumstances and habitats that are completely alien to you. As your focus remains fixed on surviving the endless onslaughts of life, you miss what the Master is doing *with* you and *for* you—strategically developing you and escorting you from one stage of blessings to the next.

To put it simply, the seed doesn't understand the vine that it's becoming. Everything that occurs in its life appears to be happenstance because all it can see is the muck and mire that it's trying to escape. It's when we are vines that we can look back at what we used to be and notice that what appeared to be accidents, incidents, and coincidence converged to produce what we are and the fruit that hangs from our branches.

---

*The seed doesn't understand the vine that
it's becoming.*

Serita and I couldn't see what the Lord was doing, but we now see that He was laying the foundation and pouring the concrete for the structure that would come later. The Master didn't require that we see and understand the blueprints He held in His hands. He only requested that we trust Him as He worked.

The vinedresser is doing the same with you.

God doesn't expect you to wrap your mind around how you should grow. He only expects your trust as you seemingly stumble your way through the process, because growth is riddled with constant change and correction. It's through the stumblings in our lives that the Master takes us from the seed stages to the fruit-bearing stages. And it's through our own planning, stubbornness, and need to have our way that we derail ourselves.

For example, I am a planner. My family and friends will tell you that I am ten years ahead of wherever we are on the calendar. But I have learned—and you must, too—that all our plans and desires must take a back seat to the creative process God is orchestrating for our lives. It's good to plan, but you must leave room for God to cultivate your growth. Sometimes we get in the way or delay what He wants to do. We think we know what's best and what will be the most productive use of our time and resources, but the truth is that only the Master Vintner knows the perfect time in our lives for His work to be done.

Think back on your life and all the events, highs and lows and in-betweens, that have brought you to where you are now. Look around your life right now, and begin taking stock of the situations where you're struggling and striving. They can be terrible and tumultuous, or pleasant and peaceful, but more likely part of the mundane fabric that often upholsters our daily lives. Whatever their nature may be, I assure you that there is purpose in your stumbling.

Let go of whatever burden of regret you may harbor within your heart. The failed relationships, the lost opportunities, the wasted money, the unhealthy lifestyle choices, the reckless decisions—surrender them and trust that they happened for a reason you may never understand but must still accept as part of your journey.

Because here's what you must realize: God did not arrange every single step of your life to this point to leave the weight of your future solely in your own hands. He has not brought you this far to culminate in a cul-de-sac of constraint. He provides a blessing and lesson in what seems to be random, because it's all part of your cultivation. With God, nothing is wasted. He redeems even our darkest moments by allowing us to become a prism of His light.

God did not arrange every single step of your life to this point to leave the weight of your future solely in your own hands.

We can choose to move along with God, allowing Him to navigate and take us into unforeseen areas of unexpected growth. Or we can become frustrated and throw tantrums like toddlers, insisting on our way and the attitudes of entitlement and victimhood to which we cling. But even in those moments of self-ish indulgence, everything we do only proves that we are in desperate need of cultivation by Him. And if we repeatedly reject His divine intentions and revolt against His methods, we will force Him to resort to even more drastic measures to develop us.

God never gives up on you.

The Discomfort of Dung

Even when we choose to cooperate with God and to seek Him in all that we do, it does not ensure our comfort or convenience, because even when God continues to move and cultivate us, there are times when we require more nutrients to grow. Instead of infusing us with more life, the Vinedresser steps in with more rubbish and refuse, the miracle of mulch, because our new life comes only on the heels of something that died.

It would seem to us that our growth would begin in places of comfort, but that's counterproductive and backward to a Master who has died and given rise to a harvest the likes and size of which the world has never seen. To Him, our comfort is the prison that produces more cycles of stagnancy. Therefore, He disrupts our convenience and stirs up trouble to stimulate what has gone dormant.

Let me give you another example. Like many people, I work out with a trainer in order to keep my body healthy and fit for the fights of life. Now I would love for you to look at me and think that I'm the epitome of physical fitness and need no assistance on my journey to healthy living, but I have to work to win this battle against gravity and keep everything in its proper place. After working out for a long time, I finally realized that the results I sought in the midst of my comfortable regimen constantly evaded me. It wasn't until I was forced to step outside of my comfort zone that muscle growth and fat loss finally occurred.

As much as I didn't enjoy the pain of pushing myself, I quickly learned the value of training on a stability ball. To perform the movements, you must engage every muscle in your core. Muscles I didn't even know I had began working simply because I was in an awkward position that required them to work to find balance. Their strain, however, produced strength. I could have completed the necessary reps with more weight on a bench, but the exercise wouldn't have been as effective because of the amount of support for the rest of my body.

In other words, our convenience causes atrophy of what needs to grow, while, on the other hand, we thrive in the unfamiliar and unstable atmosphere of cultivation. This is just not a physical principle for stronger muscles but also the premise of spiritual growth. In His parable about the fig tree that wouldn't yield fruit, Jesus said that the Owner of the vineyard had searched for fruit from the tree for three years. Finding none, He ordered the vinedresser to cut it down. "But he replied to him, 'Leave it alone, sir, [just] this one more year, till I dig around it and put manure [on the soil]. Then perhaps it will bear fruit after this; but if not, you can cut it down *and* out" (Luke 13:8–9 AMPC).

Our convenience causes atrophy of what needs to grow, while, on the other hand, we thrive in the unfamiliar and unstable atmosphere of cultivation.

If your life is suddenly unstable and you notice an increase in the amount of mess and manure placed upon you, pay close attention. It is a signal from the Lord for you to look carefully for the areas where your growth might have stalled. The vinedresser applies an extra amount of dung to a plant that stubbornly refuses to grow, because the messes of life serve as the vitamins required for healthy fruit. The irony, of course, is that what we abhor is simultaneously what we need the most. It's the Master's expert use of trials, tribulations, and trouble to stimulate us that force us to produce the best grapes for making wine.

Miserable Meditations

Most of us underestimate all that the Master has invested in us. The time, the location, the planting, and even the suffering serve His singular purpose. If the Vinedresser would go to such lengths to grow us and help us produce fruit, why do we think we are unable to handle the trouble He allows to come our way? Why do we believe that any instance of hardship and pain in our lives is the end? If He is omnipotent, omnipresent, and omniscient—and He is—then we have to accept that He has constructed us with full knowledge of the obstacles in our paths.

Nevertheless, when trouble comes, we so often ignore His perfect plan and entertain the doubting questions of the enemy. We allow our inner critics to become bullhorns of belittling comments and biting critiques of our relationship with God, doubting that He loves us and wants what is best for us. In fact, our spiritual enemy loves to undermine our faith in God by questions such as these:

> *How could God know what he's doing if you're still sick?*
> *You've been living check-to-check all your life, trying to get ahead. How could there be divine wisdom in that?*
> *If God knows everything and is all-powerful, then He could have stopped the cancer from spreading. Do you really think He knows what He's doing?*
> *Why would God let you lose your job after all you've done for that place? What good can possibly come from being unemployed?*
> *How could God allow that relationship to end? If He loved you, would He really want you to be by yourself?*

If you've ever had thoughts like this, you are not alone. I, too, have been lost in the mental maze of such miserable meditations. These questions haunt us all in the midst of the labyrinth of laments. We wallow in doubt and worry and allow ourselves to be consumed by fear and anxiety. Our complaints and doubts, however, come from an individual that has forgotten that God has specifically tailored our struggles so that we would produce succulent fruit.

The thought that we've been chosen for the pain confuses us because we believe that God is stumbling into our future just like we are. We assume that he's unaware of what's just around the corners of life, that His point of view is as limited as our own. We don't immediately warm up to a God who would say, "Ah! Now, this broken home is the perfect spot for him to become an excellent father!" For what loving God would put the object of His love through such trauma? It's when we're planted in pain and pressed by His purpose that we shake our fists and demand that He immediately cease His plan and assist with ours.

We waste valuable time and energy any time we think we know better than God—even when we can't make sense of the circumstances in which we feel buried. *Especially* when we cannot see anything except darkness and can only smell the stench of decay.

During such moments, we must trust that something is growing. Something is being birthed in the invisible realities we likely cannot see. How do I know this? Because the Lord has made it clear: "For I know the plans I have for you," declares the LORD, "plans to prosper you and not to harm you, plans to give you hope and a future." (Jer. 29:11 NIV).

We must trust that something is growing.

The presence of pain in your life isn't a prophecy of your destruction. Rather, your troubles are a sign that He is preparing you for your arrival at a bright and cheerful ascent. You are in the process of sprouting new life. But I understand the difficulty in simply trusting Him. When we're burdened by distresses and overwhelmed by the urgent demands of life, we forget that our Vinedresser truly has our best interests at heart.

These are the moments when we're prone to spiritual amnesia and must choose to fight in faith and claim what God has promised us. Even in the midst of our kicking and screaming to be released from the intentional cultivation of our lives, God steps in with a promise that has brought unyielding comfort to me in those moments when my imminent ruin was staring me in the face: "Fear not [there is nothing to fear], for I am with you; do not look around you in terror *and* be dismayed, for I am your God. I will strengthen *and* harden you to difficulties, yes, I will help you; yes, I will hold you up *and* retain you with My [victorious] right hand of rightness *and* justice" (Isa. 41:10 AMPC).

Notice what God says in addition to telling us there is nothing to fear and to not look around in apprehension and alarm. He reminds us that He will strengthen and harden us against the very agony, anguish, and anxiety that would befall us. He speaks knowing that we will encounter all this and more, but He also promises that He will develop within us the strength and fortitude to stand firm in the face of it, survive it, and thrive in the midst of it.

Displaced for a Divine Destination

You're tired and feel you're almost at your end. You've been displaced and uprooted from everything familiar in your life, and you're looking for anything to help you stabilize yourself against the uncertainty of tomorrow. This is the season when you stop looking for exterior assistance and allow God to develop and stimulate the dormant muscles of your core. This is the season when your endurance, resolve, and fortitude are enhanced. Though you've done everything you can to get the Master's attention in hopes that He would relent from His plan to crush you, I assure you that He is not out to destroy you. On the contrary, He's out to remake you, remodel you, and renew you. And He has given His word that your momentary discomfort will bring about the most profitable end.

The Father hasn't transplanted you and invested all the time and energy into growing you only to turn around and abandon you. He has placed you in the field that is uniquely equipped with the sunlight, rain, and even the dung you need to become a vine capable of bearing fruit. This field isn't your cemetery. It's the controlled environment the Master is using to cultivate you.

If we truly see Christ as the first fruits of something new and wonderful in the earth, then are willing to follow His example? Do we really perceive Him as the vine from which we spring and have life? If we, the branches, are reconnected back to the Father, who is the Husbandman, through Christ, our True Vine, in such a way that we now bear His image, it makes sense that we would undergo the same maturation process. If we follow that line of thought, we must be planted in life's dirty places, because Jesus was planted as a seed—by coming to our world in human form—with the intent that He would rise and give new life to everyone who is birthed from Him. In order for us to be born again, Jesus had to be planted and die before resurrecting to new life.

Unfortunately, we aren't allowed the luxury of having clarified hindsight of the ordeals that befall us until they have passed. We have to trust that the Husbandman knows what He is doing. While accepting that my daughter was pregnant and my mother was gone, I still had a litany of questions that I asked the Father. He remained silent for a while, and that caused me to seek him even more. I had to walk by faith and not by sight, which is what He asks of all of us.

Please understand that it is from the depths of dark and dirty places in our lives that we scream for God's attention and help while misunderstanding that, just like with a natural seed, it is the microbes in the soil of life that eat away at our efforts to protect ourselves from harm. Right when you've lost all hope, you see something you have never witnessed before.

When you resolved within yourself that maybe, just maybe, where you are is your assigned lot in life, God remains vocally silent but reminds you of His promise by showing you the light you have never seen. Breaking through the filthy soil of where you were placed in life, you sprout and rise to continue seeing another world of possibilities and say the famous words of David: "It is good for me that I have been afflicted, that I may learn Your statutes" (Ps. 119:71 AMPC).

An unplanted seed is nothing more than constrained potential. We love the thought of being gifted and having the ability to do something great, but we don't smile so brightly when we are placed in the refining processes of life. But aren't these two intimately connected? How can we have one without the other? We cannot rightfully ask the Master Husbandman to skip out on the development of our lives simply because we are uncomfortable with being alone in dark places.

An unplanted seed is nothing more than constrained potential.

What if the dark places in your life are essential to the cultivation of your full potential?

What is a seed if it's not planted? Think of the beauty, purpose, destiny, and provision that is kept from the world when we lock a seed away in order that it remain dormant. To keep a seed from being planted is to condemn that seed to never realize its full potential. It is a fact that seeds are meant to be covered and die. No matter who we are, where we are in life, or where we've come from, we must begin to appreciate the ugly stages of our inception. When we allow the Lord to shift our mindset, we begin to appreciate Jesus' words even more: "Very truly I tell you, unless a kernel of wheat falls to the ground and dies, it remains only a single seed. But if it dies, it produces many seeds" (John 12:24).

Everything that has ever happened to you happened for a reason. If we look back at the sprout that pushed itself through the ceiling of dirt above it, we arrive at the conclusion that we will understand the reasons behind our adversity when we arrive at the fruit-bearing stage. For when does a pot know exactly what its purpose is? Is it not when the potter is done forming and molding it?

Those areas and times in which the death of a dream, an assignment, or vision seems to stalk your every move are nothing more than entrances into the next realm of your life. Do not run from them. Embrace them, because the proverbial death of what you are trying to keep alive will enrich the growth and lives of others. They form the soil and mulch that generate meaning from your mistakes.

Without nutrients in the ground of its formation,

the seed cannot be planted. From one seed comes a vine. From the vine comes the fruit. From the fruit come even more seeds that give rise to even more plants. Just as Jesus was buried and from Him continue to come millions of new spiritual plants that bear marvelous grapes for making eternal wine, there are thousands of seeds that will come from you being planted. Transformation requires sacrifice, and I wonder if you have mislabeled the Husbandman's planting of you as Him condemning you to a graveyard. Far be it from the Eternal One to be so finite and temporary.

I encourage you to allow God's prison of purpose in your life to do what it was intended to do: develop you into a strong vine. It's your location of cultivation. But when God escorts you out of your season of pain, be sure to leave behind the sorrow, bitterness, and anger, just like Nelson Mandela. After all, what good would it be for the Vinedresser to take you through the entire process only for you to give rise to mediocre fruit for sour wine?

Wherever you are, whatever your dirty place might be, look around you and allow the Master to adjust your thinking. After all, God is not done with you yet. You are a seed designed to sprout. *Your fruit is becoming His wine.*

CHAPTER 4

Pruning Is Not Punishment

We shall draw from the heart of suffering itself the means of inspiration and survival.
—*Winston Churchill*

I was more nervous than usual as I prepared to speak. Usually, I can quell the butterflies with a few quiet moments alone in prayer, but this night I felt adrenaline course through my body as I listened to the audience of almost one million people buzz with excitement. Back in the green room awaiting my introduction, which was my cue to take the stage, I couldn't believe the privilege I had to be in Nigeria. It is a country with which I have a special affinity, one that is deeply spiritual in nature.

Just as I heard the crowd roar, my phone vibrated, having already been silenced. I glanced at the caller ID in the briefest of seconds and noticed it was my wife. Now, I knew that she knew I was about to speak to one of the largest audiences ever, so I couldn't imagine why she would be calling me. Without thinking, I answered in a whisper. "Hello? I'm about to go on—"

"It's Jamar," my wife said, breathlessly. "He...he's had a heart attack."

"A *heart attack*?" I echoed. My voice rose from a whisper to a roar as others standing around me looked in my direction. The line crackled with the hum of static as my mind raced to process what it could not accept. She proceeded to tell me the grim details. Our oldest son, a strapping, strong young man in his early twenties, had suffered chest pains from cardiac arrest. He now hovered on the brink of consciousness in the cardiac intensive care unit after emergency surgery.

This wasn't supposed to happen.

Never could I have imagined someone so young, strong, and healthy falling from an ailment that we tend to believe is reserved for middle-aged workaholics and senior citizens. While I was about to preach the first of several sermons I had been invited to deliver at a church there in Lagos, my son was writhing in pain in the hospital. As doctors and nurses attempted to stabilize his condition in the emergency room, Jamar suffered a second heart attack and was rushed into surgery to remove the blockage and insert a stent in his collapsed artery.

As I ended the call with my wife, my mind shifted to the only goal that mattered: getting home to be with my son. After a flurry of phone calls, along with a sincere apology to my hosts, I rushed to the airport, aware that it was about to close for the night. Fortunately, my hosts and some other kind friends contacted the authorities at the airport and informed them of my urgency. They were kind enough to make sure that my flight could take off. Only when I was on the plane gliding into the dark African sky did I feel like I began to breathe again. Only then did I say the first of many, many prayers, begging God to spare my son's life, to heal his broken heart, and to comfort my own.

Only then did I begin to wonder why this happened.

Why We Suffer

When we suffer, we seek answers. Perhaps it's the desire to regain some semblance of control over circumstances that remind us of our utter powerlessness in certain realities. Or maybe it's just our human longing to believe that everything happens for a reason, that all the details of our lives should fit together like puzzle pieces revealing significance beyond anything we can see from our surface perspective.

For those of us who trust in the goodness and sovereignty of God, this compelling need to understand why certain events occur is no less stringent. "And we know that in all things God works for the good of those who love Him, who have been called according to His purpose," the Bible tells us (Rom. 8:28). Even as we cling to the promises of divine truth, we scrutinize our natural world for answers that can only have supernatural solutions. Somehow we inherently believe that if we can understand the motivation and contextualization of our crisis, then we can contain it, reduce it, eliminate it.

Rarely do we get the understanding or revelatory insight we crave in the midst of our suffering, however. From my own experience and the privilege of walking alongside others during their most painful losses, I've learned that grieving is not the time to look for answers. It takes all your energy just to survive the turbulence of the loss. And truth be told, there is no philosophical or theological comprehension that can adequately articulate the pain radiating from one whose soul cries out in silent screams.

Rarely do we get the understanding or revelatory insight we crave in the midst of our suffering.

When I finally entered the hospital room where my beloved son lay, nearly twelve hours after my wife had called me, I did not see the frame of the over six-foot-tall man connected to tubes and monitors there. I saw my baby, my little boy, my beloved son. I saw a kaleidoscope of the many moments in which his grinning face looked up at me, the times when his tiny hand slipped into mine, the occasions when his vibrancy could not be contained.

Later, after Jamar began making a full recovery, I wondered if all parents feel that way when they see their children suffer. I imagined the awe-inspiring shock and soul-numbing sadness of Mary, the mother of Jesus, when she looked up from the foot of the cross and saw her beloved son nailed to crossbeams of rough wood next to two criminals. Did she see the Lion of Judah, the consolation of Israel, the Messiah, the Savior of the world come to forgive us of our sins?

Or did she see the infant she had birthed in a stable, the baby she had wrapped in swaddling clothes and laid in a manger?

Or perhaps she saw the toddler who had played in the yard in Nazareth, laughing and singing, calling out to her in the exuberance of childhood. Maybe it was the boy growing in wisdom and stature and in favor with God and man, smelling of sweat and sawdust from His earthly father's carpentry. Perhaps it was all of these. For, you see, our Savior was her son.

There she stands at the foot of the cross, eyes affixed to the horrific sight while everything in her wanted to turn away from it. As they executed her son by crucifixion, I wonder if others could see her anguish leaking through the pores of His skin or her love dripping out of His wounds as He bled. Mary knew she would never be the same again because they had crucified her son.

I have seen pictures of the *Pietà*, Michelangelo's famous marble statue of Mary holding the lifeless body of her son after He was taken down from the cross. The sculpture is a stunning work of art, larger than life-size in its famous corner of St. Peter's Basilica in Rome. But I suspect the true artistry of this magnificent work is the way the sculptor captured the essence of the ineffable emotion in a grieving mother's gaze. She had raised him to be a good boy, a good man, a man after God's own heart, and that's what got him killed.

How is it that the righteous suffer? Throughout the history of humankind we have wrestled with the why behind our losses. Across the pages of the Bible, we see this question posed again and again. As the Psalmist contemplates why the wicked seem to prosper while the faithful suffer, he says, "All day long I have been afflicted, and every morning brings new punishments... When I tried to understand all this, it troubled me deeply *till I entered the sanctuary of God*; then I understood their final destiny" (Ps. 73: 14, 16–17, my emphasis).

Answering this question is crucial to your recovery from life's crushing blows.

For, you see, the difference between pruning and punishment is in intention. It's not figuring out how one suffers something different from someone else—it's looking at *why* they suffer. Both sufferings look and feel almost the same. For Mary gazing up at Golgotha, she saw two men being crucified beside her son, screaming, bleeding, and crying out in the delirious spasms of excruciating pain. Despite their resemblance, there was a crucial difference: two were being punished, and one was being pruned.

Buried or Planted?

God doesn't cut us to kill us but to heal us. It's the difference between experiencing the blade of a dagger in a back-alley attack and the blade of a scalpel in an operating room. After I endured back surgery to alleviate the pressure various discs were exerting on my spine, my doctor told me that the pain of recovery is so intense because the body responds the same as if it had been assaulted by stab wounds even when the finest surgeon has delicately cut into the flesh to save your life.

God doesn't cut us to kill us but to heal us.

But the intent of each produces a distinctly different outcome. If you suffer a knife wound in a mugging and it goes untreated, then your body will deteriorate, become infected, and die. On the other hand, when the surgeon's work makes reparation, your body's pain leads to healing and recovery. The difference in intent does not nullify the similarities in pain. But it does change the direction of your focus as you answer the why.

This difference in intention is reflected in the way we perceive our immersion into the present pain. We can recognize that the seeds of our greatness, which God has imbued into our very being, are being buried in order to take root, sprout, and produce fruit. Or we can assume we're being buried alive, suffocated by the severity of our circumstances. Being planted and being buried may feel similar—if not identical—but the intention leads to very different outcomes.

Here's what makes the difference in shifting our perspective: in the midst of suffering, we must allow ourselves to find faith without denying truth. We must experience the freedom to express our pain and discomfort without becoming paralyzed by our wounds. But we must also enjoy the liberation that only hope can bring, the hope born of understanding that we are not being punished but merely being pruned. We are being cut only so we can grow stronger and straighter, truer and more trustworthy.

Job knew this strange paradox. His very name has become synonymous with suffering and oppressive calamity. Even as the burning stench of rubble from his lost homes and deceased children filled his nostrils, Job refused to blame himself or to accept the counsel of others who assumed he was being punished by God. Job knew he did not deserve to experience the kind of loss being heaped on him, the kind of loss compounded by each new crisis unfolding around him. This was his truth.

But Job also knew he had put his trust in God. He believed God loved him and cared about him and had not allowed such loss in Job's life as some kind of sadistic punishment. The beauty of the book of Job is the way it provides a field guide for the rest of us. Notice how Job manages to express his truth even as he clings to his trust in the Lord:

> Keep silent and let me speak; then let come to
> me what may.
>   Why do I put myself in jeopardy and take
> my life in my hands?
>   Though He slay me, yet will I hope in Him;
> I will surely defend my ways to His face.
>   Indeed, this will turn out for my
> deliverance, for no godless person would dare
> come before Him! (Job 13:13–16)

Job refuses to mouth the words of some glib platitude or trite condolence. He allows himself to be true to where he is in the process. This reinforces what I have observed in grieving families: those who embrace their anguish and cry out tend to heal more fully than those who try to pretend they're okay. With the magnitude of Job's losses, however, there was no way to pretend that anything was okay. He had lost it all—his wealth, his home, his family, his friends, his health, *everything.*

But Job refuses to believe this is all there is. He will not give up and accept defeat. He can't believe his life will end in ruin. Truth and trust hold hands in Job's soul, and this is the union we must explore in order to push beyond our view of circumstances and into a bigger, divine perspective. God's pruning, those events He allows us to endure even though they cause us pain and discomfort, are never intended as punishment! Why would God send His only son to die on the cross for our sins if He planned to continue to punish us? We are all sinful and can never pay the debt we owe—which is why Jesus did it for us.

Truth and trust hold hands in Job's soul, and this is the union we must explore in order to push beyond our view of circumstances and into a bigger, divine perspective.

God allows such pruning just as a loving father disciplines a child so that the child will mature and reach her full potential. We're told, "Do not despise the LORD's discipline, and do not resent His rebuke, because the LORD disciplines those He loves, as a father the son He delights in" (Prov. 3:11–12). When my mother made me miss the school dance because I had not completed my chores as I had promised, she was doing me a supreme favor. She was teaching me to honor my promises in order to reap their rewards.

Most parents try to teach their children the same kinds of lessons. Because they love their children and want them to succeed—and because they want this more than they want their child to be comfortable and content in the moment—mothers and fathers look at a bigger picture, their child's future, and the desired outcome. If we in our flawed abilities and weaknesses can parent in this manner, then surely our Heavenly Father in His holy perfection can do so much more! Jesus said, "Which of you, if your son asks for bread, will give him a stone? Or if he asks for a fish, will give him a snake? If you, then, though you are evil, know how to give good gifts to your children, how much more will your Father in heaven give good gifts to those who ask Him!" (Matt. 7:9–11).

Pruned for Greater Growth

Sharing this truth with you is intended to help you view your wounds from a new perspective. I'm a people person, through and through. If you talk to my family and friends, without a doubt they will tell you that I love people. After all, our relationships are our greatest resource, and my effectiveness as a leader finds its foundations in the proximity of my heart to the sheep I'm called to shepherd. Indeed, I rejoice when I see God's people being blessed.

I'm convinced that the most poignant and powerful moments in our lives, however, happen when God takes us through the instructional and developmental seasons of suffering. As a result, I'm drawn to the lost and hurting. Yes, I'm an encourager and seek to inspire people, but my gift of exhortation sprouted in a dark place and was cut and trimmed by the Master's scalpel of life's difficulties.

Gravitating toward suffering and hurting people led me to counsel a young man by the name of Michael. Bright, well educated, and hardworking, Michael had his sights fixed on a promotion that was all but promised to him, and he was aware his superiors were grooming him for its assumption. Months later, instead of the company handing him papers with a new title and higher salary, Michael received a pink slip and a pat on the back and was escorted out the front door by the building's security guards.

As Michael sat on the couch in my office, he stared at me expectantly, hoping that somehow I could comfort him with divine wisdom and assuage his feelings about his predicament. Everything in me wanted to offer him words of wisdom right then and there, but the Father stopped me because there was something He wanted Michael to see—something my words would pale in comparison to.

It was a lesson I had learned the hard way myself. Back in my younger days, my brother and I had started a window and siding business that we just knew would be our ticket to success. We were both young, strong, and resilient and had just enough knowledge of home construction to believe we could make our business succeed. We borrowed against my car and proceeded to incur numerous startup costs even as new customers dwindled.

It didn't take long for our business to go belly-up. I lost my car, and we were forced to ask our mother for money to cover the checks we had written that were suddenly bouncing all over town. She had to dip into her savings to loan us the money, and we felt even more ashamed of our failure.

If our business had succeeded, however, then Potter's House would not exist. I would probably be an itinerant pastor working for Supreme Windows in Charleston, West Virginia. At the time I thought it was the end of my life, that I had failed before I even got started. I lost my livelihood, my transportation, and my confidence.

Looking back years later, I realized that I had temporarily allowed my little-brother complex to get in the way of my divine destiny. My life's direction had been momentarily subverted by my idolization of my big brother and my desire to please him instead of doing what God was calling me to do. In the agony of the moment, I could not see my way through to the brightness of where I would one day arrive.

In the agony of the moment, I could not see my way through to the brightness of where I would one day arrive.

But how to convey this truth to my young friend with the heavy heart sitting across from me? I yearned to break the silence that hovered in the air so heavily but felt compelled to hold back. Not even our breathing and the cool air whispering through the vents pierced the stillness. With the thick sullenness of the bereaved, Michael dropped his head and stared at the carpeting. Then, as if the truth finally hit him, he returned his gaze to me and exclaimed, "Why *me*? I did everything right! Everything I've ever worked for is *gone*!"

At that moment, the dam of Michael's emotions burst, and the weeping he had held at bay for so long poured out of him. He was collapsing under the weight of the loss of his main source of income and the resulting fears and anguish about his family's possible future—a future that now remained only a fleeting possibility. Yet, there still lingered a point the Lord wanted Michael to discover. I handed him a box of tissues and allowed him all the time he needed to collect himself.

Michael wasn't without sin, but he was correct—he had done everything right. He was the best at his job. He volunteered at the church. He paid his tithes. He was an upstanding man, a leader among leaders. None of this warranted him being beyond human heartache. Because God loved Michael more than he could see in the moment. Michael felt like he was being punished unfairly when he was actually being pruned by God's gracious hand.

Why *Not* You?

I've been escorted to the breaking points of life many times before, and what added to my confusion was the realization that the most grievous points of my journey followed closely behind moments of extraordinary joy. I remember when God began adjusting my perspective of the pain we feel during the pruning seasons of life. My family was experiencing unprecedented blessings, the church was doing extremely well, and great opportunities for ministry continued to present themselves.

Then the economic collapse of 2008 shattered my happiness. Within a matter of months, I went from witnessing a harvest season that drove me to my knees in praise to finding myself in a season where every fruitful endeavor and vine was agonizingly chopped down to the roots. While I had already been subsidizing the payroll for our church staff, I no longer had the resources to cover dozens of employees. We had to lay off forty people.

What could have possibly been the purpose of allowing the church to be fat with a surplus and then, suddenly, to be peeled down to the bones? It wasn't until I was gazing out of those all too familiar windows during one of those lonely dark nights of the soul when I finally allowed myself to ask God, "Why me, Lord?"

He shocked me with his response in three simple words: *Why not you?*

The Master's sharp and direct question highlighted

a mistake I didn't even realize I had made. I had incorrectly assumed that I, my family, and others around us had sinned and not repented of it, as if we had to have provoked His judgment in some way. Kindly, the Lord reminded me of *when* pruning takes place.

Pruning always happens after the harvest.

There I was, questioning God's timing and wisdom in my life when His schedule was perfect. God's pruning of the branches of blessings in my life on the heels of a massive harvest were in direct keeping with the very words of the Master Himself: "Every branch in Me that does not bear fruit He takes away; and every *branch* that bears fruit He prunes, that it may bear more fruit" (John 15:2 NKJV).

Notice that Jesus did not say He prunes *some* of the branches that bear fruit. Rather, He cuts back *every* fruit-bearing branch. God's pruning of me was not because I did something wrong. I felt the searing pain of the cutting back of my branches because I did something *right*—I bore fruit.

So before you ask, "Why me?" may I dare to ask, "Why *not* you?"

So before you ask, "Why me?" may I dare to ask, "Why not you?"

God has confirmed you on the back end of a harvest season as you stand in the middle of your vines that now have no fruit. There are others who, like you, can point to their history and cry aloud to the Father, "I've done everything right!" But your behavior does not make you immune to the same wounds every other productive branch receives. Look around you to the other vines in the field and see that they, too, have suffered cutting at the hands of the Master. You are part of a select group of people who have been chosen by the Vinedresser to be pruned because you've done something that other branches have not: *fulfilled your purpose!*

The Pain of Public Pruning

When we are being pruned by the Master, He nonetheless presents us with a choice. On one hand, we are experiencing the inescapable trauma of the Lord trimming from us what we thought makes us valuable. On the other, we have the desire for our comfort that the enemy uses to entice us away from the glorious future.

Jesus, too, had to choose. He made His choice when He taught a lesson that flew in the face of the religiosity of the Sadducees, Pharisees, and their followers. After revealing the spiritual meaning and reality of the Passover bread and wine, many of His own followers turned away from Him. The Jesus who performed over thirty miracles was the same Jesus that began losing people simply because He fulfilled His purpose. As some of his disciples left Him, He turned to the twelve and asked, "Will you also go away?" (John 6:67 AMPC).

Even after the harvest of the many souls that sought and put their faith in Him, the Master found Himself being pruned by the Father. The question that Jesus asked His disciples is the same one He asks each of us. As the Vinedresser approaches with His pruning hook, foretelling the somber and sorrowfulness of the season, we have a choice. We can stay in the process and be pruned as He fashions us to look more like him, or we can choose our immediate, temporary comfort and forfeit our future.

Please understand, I know firsthand that such cutting is gruesome and ghastly, but when we are choosing between remaining finite and becoming infinite, isn't the preferable option clear? We are the contemporary disciples who must choose to accept the fiery agony that results from being cut by the Vinedresser's pruning shears or miss out on the joy, peace, and contentment that comes from fulfilling the purpose for which our Creator designed us.

We are the contemporary disciples who must choose to accept the fiery agony that results from being cut by the Vinedresser's pruning shears or miss out on the joy, peace, and contentment that comes from fulfilling the purpose for which our Creator designed us.

So, what will you do when he asks you, "Will you leave also?"

Looking at my life, you can tell the choice I made. Yes, the pain was dreadful, and some days it still stings, but I promise you there hasn't been a day when I question whether it was worth it. Pruning is not punishment— it's the pathway to God's power in your life.

Yesterday's Fruit, Tomorrow's Wine

One thing I'm certain of is that God loves me. I've been through too much in my life and seen how the Father has taken care of me to say that he doesn't have his hand on me. I can hardly speak about how I've seen God move in my life without becoming overwhelmed. I realize that some people don't feel that way about God. They look at their lives and can see only negativity that forces them to ask, "If God loves me, why does life keep hurting me? Why do I keep losing everything that's valuable?"

Really? Is what you lost that valuable?

In this season, at this age, in this stage of your life, the fruit you've held on to has been culled, and you're desperately trying to stop the bleeding. On the outside, your blessings have been taken from you, but the exterior pangs you feel are accompanied by the inward agony for what you cannot reclaim. But the Master has not placed value where we have. Whereas we long for what has been taken, the Master is overjoyed with what remains. Could it be that the Lord hides next season's harvest in what we have left?

Your miracle is never in what you lost—it's in what you have left!

If you're down to a handful of meal, that's all you need. If you're down to two fish and five loaves of bread, that's all you need! Like the widow in the Old Testament (2 Kings), you can be down to one last jar of oil, but the Lord has created more capacity for you to pour out, improve upon, and increase what you have left. The Lord, then, would have you begin looking at what remains and cease grieving over what you lost. After all, if you needed what the Master took from you, do you really believe the Lord would have sought to take it?

For where God is taking you, you don't need the

weight and refuse of yesterday's bread. The Master has an expected end for your life, and the trip doesn't require the extra baggage of last season's blessings. If the Lord, in all his wisdom, took from you what would weigh you down during the next leg of your journey, why would you seek ways to regain it? In pruning you, the Lord is assisting you in circumspectly and precisely tailoring your life down to carry only what you need to get you where he wants you to go, because he knows that the blessing of last season's harvest can become a trap and graveyard for your future.

Are you willing to leave behind yesterday's fruit so you can embrace the wine of tomorrow's new season?

I'm writing to those of you who find yourselves awestruck by the damage left behind by a Master who dared to cut you. Though it appears that everything you built has been taken from you, the Lord has strategically left a remnant that will give rise to more fruit next season. It's the remnant that is most valuable to the Vinedresser, for there is life in what remains.

Though it appears that everything you built has been taken from you, the Lord has strategically left a remnant that will give rise to more fruit next season.

It's easy to roll over and submit to the lies that you'll never get up, that you'll never get better, that you'll never see the blessings of God in your life again. Those beliefs come when we lose sight of the fact that God has *promised* that we would be pruned. It's a fact that any leader, CEO, parent, teacher, mentor, or person of destiny can expect. There will be loss. In the face of the pruning that has been promised, we forget the affirmation that lies within its purpose: "And every *branch* that bears fruit He prunes, that it may bear more fruit" (John 15:2 NKJV).

The only reason he has allowed what we had to be taken from us is because he has promised that he holds even better for us. He culls from us the blessings of yesterday to prevent our ensnarement to the past at the expense of the wine of our future. To the utmost, I believe that God never allows anything to be seized and torn from us if he didn't have something better to put right back in its place.

Nearly a year later, a different Michael strolled into my office with a sheepish grin on his face. Not everything in his life was back to normal, but there was joy about him. Anxiety about the well-being of his family and future was gone, having been replaced with a renewed sense of purpose and destiny. Just a few months after Michael's employment ended, he stepped into entrepreneurship. Looking back, he could now see that his unemployment was the freedom he needed to begin doing on his own terms what he loved the most. The pruning that once hurt Michael so badly turned out to be one of the best things that ever happened to him.

The promise of pruning should never bring sorrow and heartache to anyone attached to Christ. Rather, God's approach with his pruning shears should inspire confidence and joy because we are being prepared to grow and give birth to something even better. If there is any doubt about God's love for you, the blessings He's given you and his preparation of you for the next season is positive proof that not only does the Vinedresser love you, but there is also fruit and life after pruning.

If you are being pruned as you read this book, if your heart is aching and your soul is suffering, then I ask that you trust God as He prepares you for what lies ahead. He loves you and will never abandon you or harm your ultimate well-being—even when the slice of devastating circumstances cuts you deeply. Have confidence in God's ability to do the impossible and to surprise you with His joy, comfort you with His peace, and fulfill you with His purpose.

Pruning is not punishment—it's the beginning of your greatest season yet!

CHAPTER 5

Blood of the Vine

I have found the paradox, that if you love until it hurts, there can be no more hurt, only more love.
                                    —*Mother Teresa*

This past Independence Day my wife and I celebrated the holiday by hosting a cookout for our children, grandchildren, and extended family. While little ones splashed in the pool next to the gentle, cascading waterfall in our garden, adults lounged in wicker chairs nearby. Sunshine flickered through green, leafy branches of the many shade trees surrounding us as we grilled burgers, dogs, and ribs, and all the fixin's, like countless other families in our country that day.

As everyone talked and mingled, indulged in another scoop of potato salad, and savored our time together, I sat back and smiled to myself, taking it all in. I sipped my glass of sweet iced tea and silently gave thanks for the privilege of living in a free country. My prayer included my deep, heartfelt thanks for the millions of men and women who serve, protect, and defend our great nation, many of whom have sacrificed their lives.

Then, like a dark cloud suddenly blocking the sun, a shadow fell across my heart. That day we celebrated the founding of our United States of America and the many freedoms established by our Founding Fathers and Mothers in our Declaration of Independence. And yet…those freedoms emerged out of a social, cultural, and economic system dependent on the backs of slaves and usurped from our land's original native inhabitants. Those freedoms, as revolutionary and well intended as they were, did not liberate all, only some.

So why should we be celebrating? Has the smell of smoked ribs and the exuberance of children jumping into swimming pools anesthetized our ability to remember the suffering of others, those who are not free?

That evening, as we oohed and ahhed over dazzling showers of red, white, and blue fireworks, I couldn't shake the feeling that we should not be celebrating while so many people continued to struggle, suffer, and strive toward freedoms so many of us take for granted. People incarcerated without hope of rehabilitation or restoration. People recuperating from injuries sustained because of the color of their skin. People burying loved ones killed because of the quick-trigger prejudices of those around them.

We celebrate even as they suffer. Too often, the sufferers are often forgotten by the celebrators. But can we truly celebrate freedom if even one person remains enslaved by prejudice, racism, sexism, poverty, or lack of opportunity in the pursuit of happiness?

My heart grieved that day as I recalled something Martin Luther King Jr. said, that no one is free until we are all free. We celebrate our great nation and its many freedoms each Independence Day, but we must not overlook those whose souls scream out in silence, mourning the injustice, apathy, indignity, and indifference they face each day in these same fifty states. We are knit together as one country, but we threaten to unravel at the seams if we do not rely on one another as the thread of shared freedom binds us all together.

This awareness is about so much more than one day of the year. The suffering of the innocent is inherent in the acquisition of freedom. Remembering those who still suffered under independence deserves more than a refusal to celebrate, though I know some choose to deny the date and ignore the holiday. But I felt it was a teaching moment for my family and friends that since we are the juice of the crushing of our ancestors, then we must ensure that their suffering status in 1776 was not the end of the story. Yes, eventually slavery was abolished and Jim Crow was dealt a furious blow. But even to this day, there is still much to be done.

Celebrating or not celebrating a holiday isn't the fruit of such audacious atrocities of the past. Freedom is more than the keeping or removal of a statue. Freedom is the complete inclusion of opportunity and the total reform of any residual systemic imbalance so as to level the playing field of disadvantage that has existed for generations. From ghetto streets to small-town parades, from reservations to country clubs, we must let freedom ring throughout every corridor of this great country. All of us must fight every day for the liberation and justice for the sons and daughters of the slaves, the Native Americans, and all others who paid a huge price for the freedom of others.

Not just some but *all*.

Suffering must never be wasted.

Spilled blood is always redeemed.

Crushing is not the end.

Crushing is not the end.

Shared Suffering

I share these reflections not to stir up feelings of pain, guilt, anger, or shame. This is not the time to argue about who is at fault, to defend oneself and point the finger at someone else. Now is not the time for pronouncements of right and wrong—not while others continue to suffer. Now is the time to recover those who have been crushed and to recover our humanity within our own crushing.

I'm reminded of an incident years ago when I was a young man living in West Virginia. Driving through the hills along the backroads one day, I came around a curve and saw a car had crashed into a tree beyond the shoulder of the road. I pulled over and rushed to the vehicle. There I saw the driver, his head bleeding, standing next to his crumpled sedan with its shattered windshield. Unsure of what to do first, I blurted, "Should I call the police?"

"No," he said. "Call an ambulance!"

The same is true today. Our compassion has crashed when so many people in hospitals, nursing homes, prisons, rehab clinics, and reservations feel buried alive.

Suffering in isolation, they sense that others cannot bother to pause in the midst of their celebrations to remember them and their physical, mental, emotional, social, and economic struggles.

Returning to my home state of West Virginia recently, I was surprised that a place so conservative and community-oriented had become a leader in the opioid epidemic now ravaging our country. Who knew that the grocery clerks and schoolteachers were getting addicted? When did the electricians and plumbers slip into the deadly tentacles of addiction? Why did no one notice their silent screams? Why are we so slow to move into another's pain? Are those who suffer communicating on a frequency we simply cannot hear? Or do we ignore the cacophony of pain bursting through our lives every day?

Even worse than not hearing the suffering of those around us is being tone deaf. We hear, but instead of rushing to help, we judge, criticize, and condemn. I remember seeing Oprah interview a counselor on her show once. As they discussed the way we tend to ignore the suffering of others, this expert said something profound that still haunts me. She said that human beings are much better at inflicting pain than enduring pain. We had rather hurt others—even those already hurting—than feel the hurt ourselves.

The reality, however, is that we all suffer. We all

suffer losing our children to gangs, to street drugs, to addictions we don't understand. We all suffer the indignities of aging and Alzheimer's, cancer and incarceration. We all suffer the economic roller coaster of less money and more bills. We all suffer the dislocation of our dreams and the explosion that Langston Hughes described so brilliantly when our dreams are deferred again and again and again.

We are all crushed by the same blows of life.

But not everyone allows the crushing to destroy them.

Some discover the secret of making wine out of the remaining juice.

They know how the blood of the vine becomes the fruit of the cup.

Some discover the secret of making wine out of the remaining juice.

Power in the Blood

I visited my physician several weeks ago for my annual physical. While I was there, one of the attending nurses drew my blood to perform the customary screenings for diseases and other maladies. Medical professionals require a blood draw in order to see what they cannot see with the naked eye. Blood tells them just about everything they need to know in order to understand what is working and not working within the human body.

Similarly, experts in the justice system use blood analysis to determine vital information needed to solve crimes. Blood splatter analysts work in forensics departments and visit crime scenes to determine exactly what happened to a victim and the perpetrator by examining how and where the blood landed at the location. Similarly, law enforcement and forensics officers match blood from crime scenes with DNA on file to identify the guilty. And conversely, blood collected years ago continues to exonerate individuals who were wrongfully incarcerated.

It appears then, in addition to how the body uses and produces blood, that it acts as a testifying agent to actions others have not witnessed. Just like we notice in crimes, blood can act as a string that ties individuals to a certain act. No matter the time, each person involved in the crime is linked to the blood that was spilled. If we're able to determine who was present at a murder scene weeks, months, and even years later by blood testifying as to the identity of its owner, then blood becomes a witness to the past by its existence in the present.

If you compare the words *testify* and *testament*, they both have the same Latin root word, *testi*, literally meaning "witness." In the Bible we see this meaning tied to the emphasis God seems to place on the importance of blood. Time and time again, blood becomes a way to infuse life, to communicate, to reveal, to protect, to seal, to atone, and to save. For instance, in the Garden of Eden, when God sees that it is not good for man to be alone, the Lord creates woman from part of Adam's body. When Adam then states, "This is now bone of my bones and flesh of my flesh; she shall be called 'woman,' for she was taken out of man" (Gen. 2:23), he is speaking literally as well as figuratively.

The sons of Adam and Eve also discover the power of blood. Abel, having brought an acceptable sacrifice before the Lord, and Cain, offering one deemed unacceptable in God's sight, clashed as Cain's jealousy of his own brother led him to murder Abel. God's response to Cain is revealing: "The Lord said, 'What have you done? The voice of your brother's [innocent] blood is crying out to Me from the ground [for justice]'" (Gen. 4:10 AMP). The blood of the victim speaks, crying out for justice even after his life has ended.

In Exodus, when the people of Israel struggle to leave the slavery of Egypt behind, we see how the sprinkling of blood on Hebrew doorposts saved the inhabitants of the house from the wrath of the Angel of Death. The blood of slaughtered lambs shed on the altars in the temple became the means of atonement for people's sins prior to Christ's death on the cross. The contrast between these two is important because one was temporary—the bloodshed of animals for that moment's sacrifice—and the other eternal as Jesus' shed blood and resurrection forever defeated sin and death.

With the Bible divided into the Old and New Testaments, God reveals the significance of blood in both but transforms its meaning in the transition from one sacrifice to another. In the Old Testament blood is shed by innocent animals for the covering of human sin. The New Testament, however, speaks of the blood shed by a perfect Savior for *all* of humanity's sin.

Going even deeper, the Old Testament bears witness to the fall of mankind because of sin that is transferred from generation to generation through the blood. Conversely, the New Testament testifies of the redemption of mankind through the eternal blood of Christ that is transferred from person to person via the acceptance of his sacrifice poured out on their behalf.

It Is Finished

We see this pattern repeated consistently as something from the Old Testament is transformed in meaning and redeemed in purpose when it appears in the New Testament. Adam giving birth to Eve, his bride and wife, is not the first such transformation. Because Scripture makes the distinction between a first Adam and second Adam. Seeing that everything in the Old Testament is a type and shadow of the reality we see in the New Testament, it stands to reason that the shadow of Adam giving birth to his bride in the Old Testament would have a brighter and more radiant realization in the New Testament.

This dazzling revelation is the Incarnation, God sending His only Son, Jesus, to be born of a virgin in a tiny cow town called Bethlehem. Jesus became the second Adam who would give up his own flesh and blood in order that his bride, the church, could emerge as the body of Christ. But this birthing process was a bloody, brutal business. We cannot celebrate the resurrection without lingering at the crushing of Christ on the cross. And Jesus was crushed in every way— physically beaten, emotionally isolated, and spiritually bereft.

CRUSHING

We cannot celebrate the resurrection without lingering at the crushing of Christ on the cross. And Jesus was crushed in every way—physically beaten, emotionally isolated, and spiritually bereft.

Hanging there for all to see, Christ probably didn't look human, let alone recognizable to His mother and disciples sobbing at the foot of the cross below Him. His entrails were spilling out of His abdomen, and the soldiers had placed a sign reading KING OF THE JEWS above His head to add insult to the additional injury of the twisted crown of thorns piercing his brow. His body was beaten beyond all recognition, and the blood that flowed from every perforation in his anatomy coated Him in a deep shade of crimson. His image must have been beyond terrifying. Horrific. Ghastly.

Atop Golgotha, the only thing keeping His mother, Mary, within meters of the abjectly dreadful sight of His mangled body was nothing but the sheer love of a mother for her son. Standing near Mary was another Mary who loved her Savior, Mary Magdalene. And within inches of Jesus' mother was John, the disciple the Master loved so much. Several feet away, the soldiers assigned to guard the scene scoffed and cast lots for His clothing.

Gathered around the place of execution were those who failed to glimpse the cross beyond their laws, politics, and culture. Many still shopped, repaired shoes, and laid stone while Jesus lay trembling on a cross. This dichotomous tension between those who rejoice and those who mourn is seen at the cross, where Mary weeps while the soldiers jeer and joke. Their obliviousness to her pain reminds us once again that perspective can create an insensitivity to the broader view of others.

We can never celebrate without including the crushing.

For Jesus to have even made it that far was a miracle in and of itself. Excruciating pain shot through every inch of His frame. Comfort was diabolically designed to be torturously beyond reach. As the nails in His hands became too much to bear, His body shifted His weight to His legs and feet, causing even more agony because of the nails in His ankles as well.

Once the weight on His feet took its toll, Christ would pull Himself up by His nailed hands. With no way to escape the pain, He endured growing hypoxia that made each of His breaths more labored than the one before. His lack of blood was so severe that every one of His rapidly failing organs was starving for oxygen. In essence, Jesus was suffocating as a result of His extensive bodily trauma.

With a final heave of one last breath, Jesus gasped, *"It. Is. Finished!"*

When Darkness Descends

The gospels of Matthew, Mark, and Luke bear witness to a darkness falling over Jerusalem at the time of Jesus' death, and that darkness remained for a span of three hours. Some have attempted to debunk the accounts of these three disciples by attributing that darkness to some natural phenomenon, like a solar eclipse or severe weather. Seeing as how I stand on the biblical account, taking nothing from it and adding nothing to it, I am led to believe that there was something else at play that led to the heavens giving no light at the time. Because the God who decided to express this recorded darkness is the same One who controls the weather and the rotation of the earth He created.

So why the darkness of those three hours? And why bring it to our attention?

I've had to comfort plenty of parents who have prematurely lost their children. I cannot and choose not to imagine an instance of me having to give the eulogy for my sons or daughters and then burying them. It's a nightmare I do not rehearse. Nevertheless, it is one that others have had the misfortune of suffering.

I've seen their despair, heard their cries, attended the funerals, and had to counsel them through the resulting depression and suicidal thoughts. I say that to lay the groundwork for our understanding the emotional state of any parent who has lost a child. Perhaps you have. If so, you intimately know the pain associated with something so tragic.

If our emotions are given to us by our Creator, they must be modeled after His own emotions. After all, we know God laughs. He experiences joy, sorrow, and anger. The only difference between His emotions and ours that we can fully understand is that His are pure and haven't been corrupted by the stain of sin. With that being said, doesn't it stand to reason that He would experience His emotions on a level that far supersedes our own? So His sorrow at the sight of His Son dying and becoming the representation of evil that had so infected the human heart must have torn the Father apart. On top of that, the Father had to turn His back on the sin that Christ then embodied because righteousness and unrighteousness have no part with one another.

If our emotions are given to us by our Creator,
they must be modeled after His own emotions.

The Father forsook the Son He loved so that He could be reconnected back to us.

With the sorrow felt by the Almighty and His connection to every aspect of creation, I don't believe it's farfetched that all of nature would react to the death of the glorious Son. The darkening of the sun could be seen as a reflection of the Master weeping not only at what His Son became on our behalf, but also, I offer, at the fact that so few of His own people received him. The sun refusing to shine gave us tangible evidence that the light in God's eye had temporarily dimmed. Oh, yes. Surely, Jesus' sacrifice and resurrection would turn the world upside down and lead to the harvest of billions of souls throughout the rest of human history. But, at that moment, the Master, in His eternal nature, mourned the death of His beloved Boy.

Something else, however, was also happening at His death.

Jesus gave up the ghost, meaning that His soul had departed His mortal body. Though His body would soon be placed in a tomb, His eternal spirit was already at work in the supernatural. Having reached backward and forward through time to grab hold of every sin humanity would commit, Jesus had taken upon Himself the punishment and death that we deserved. By entering the grave and conquering it on behalf of everyone who would receive Him—past, present, and future—Christ forced the grave to give up its first fruits of those saints who had gone on before as a testament to His work.

Only Matthew's recording of the gospel speaks to the breaking open of tombs and the appearance of dead saints walking around Jerusalem. I've seen many pastors and teachers overlook this fact out of fear of how to explain this phenomenon, but I hold to the notion that Jesus' presence in the grave on behalf of sin-stained humanity would not only force the grave to release a smattering of the faithful from its grasp but also upset earth itself.

After all, a new kind of man was being born—something that was the embodiment of the reconnection of God with his prized creation. In tandem with his sorrow, darkness fell and the foundations of the planet shook. Nevertheless, what if we looked at the accompanying earthquake as the heaving and pushing of a womb that was struggling to birth the newness placed in it by the seed of Jesus' sacrificial death?

Let's remember that Jesus suffered on our behalf and descended into the grave so that we might ascend back to our position of righteousness in God. He broke the shackles that bound us to sin and death. As a result, the grave had to release its hold on the faithful who lived before Christ arrived. Hence the earthquake. After He would ascend, so would they. The shaking of terra firma was not just a reaction to the Master's emotional tumult. No, it had to have been the pushing out of the first fruits of the new creation wrought by the planting of the seed of a sacrificial Savior. Just as a baby crowns when his head appears and approaches departure from the womb, so, too, did the first fruits emerge.

Without the crushing there would be no crowning!

Without the crushing there would be no crowning!

Crowning from the Crushing

There are things in your life that you have placed in the ground because you have labeled them as dead. You have decreed that they don't have life and purpose. Perhaps you've walked away from a marriage or even bade farewell to your relationship with God. As your sorrow is still tangible, a thick darkness now surrounds your heart, and you are slow in returning to its gravesite because of the pain you once felt. That trauma caused a tremendous shaking in every aspect of your life, and you have taken an oath to never hope again, never dream again, never love again, and never again take a chance that life could be better.

But the very fact that life emerged from the grave as a response to Jesus' death suggests that what you've buried still has purpose. Yet, this truth is difficult for you to accept because you struggle to realize that its appearance is quite different from how you last saw it. Once corrupted with human effort and sin, it has returned wrapped in the glory of a Savior who wishes you would turn again and see the life that now inhabits it.

Whatever your passion may be—your dream, family, church, business, book——Jesus did not die just to save only you. His death was for every part of you that you had given up on. Look again. With the Master, it is being reborn as He steps out of His tomb with all power in His hands. Just like the resurrected saints that walked the streets of Jerusalem on the day of Jesus' death were the "crowning" of the birth that would come from His resurrection, that which you have buried is crowning.

The familiar shaking you are feeling does not stem from a sorrow you cannot forget. On the contrary, it's from the birthing that is taking place in your life.

Remember that seeds eventually develop shoots that emerge from the soil in which they were once trapped. That emergence, then, is the breaking forth that has caused the unsteadiness in your life. Fear not. This is not a repeat of your darkest days. The quaking you are feeling is the dawning of a new you being pushed through the veil of Christ's suffering and death to something far more joyous and grand.

The crushing of the grape not only expresses the juice from the flesh, but it also separates the unusable parts of the grape from the juice.

Have you seen what happens to grape clusters that hang too long from the branch? Eventually, their connecting stem dries up and loses sufficient strength to bear the weight of the fruit. As a result, the grapes plummet to the ground to rot, ferment, and be consumed by insects, never realizing their full potential. It's this cut-off existence that the Vintner has so endeavored to save us from in order to show us who we really are.

Succulent fruit falling to the ground and becoming nothing more sounds like the wasting of a human life that never matured into something greater than its original form. As a result, it's as if the fruit never existed. If you choose to dwell on the fruit that has already fallen and spoiled, then you miss out on letting

God redeem that fruit by making you into His wine. And it *is* your choice! You often don't choose the painful events that disrupt your life, but you always choose how you will respond.

If you choose to dwell on the fruit that has already fallen and spoiled, then you miss out on letting God redeem that fruit by making you into His wine.

You choose what you will do with your crushing.

You can ignore the suffering and deny the despairing and attempt to celebrate. You can also resign yourself to the despondency that sours when crushing seems to have no purpose. Or you can choose to enter into the tension between celebrating and suffering that crushing requires. The choice is yours.

CHAPTER 6

The Price of Crushing

Character cannot be developed in ease and quiet.
Only through experience of trial and suffering can
the soul be strengthened, ambition inspired, and
success achieved.

—*Helen Keller*

I remember the very moment I received word from the Master that I was to speak and preach for Him. If you think I saw rainbows and halos and a choir of angels singing as I erupted in grateful reception of the Lord's calling on my life, please think again! With everything in me, I ran from it. If you think Jonah ran from His calling, you would have been astonished at how quickly I dodged my assignment.

It simply didn't make sense. When God told me that I would be used to proclaim His infallible Word to the world, my personal history immediately flooded my mind. There was no way God had the right man. How could He pick someone who had such a scuffed and scarred history? If God is holy and perfect—which He is—then surely there must be some mistake for Him to choose me.

Looking back, however, I now see that God in His infinite wisdom and loving kindness knew exactly what He was doing. During the writing of this book, I celebrated my sixtieth birthday, and now with over forty years in ministry, I see how God's plan often thrives in the lives of those who don't seem fit for the calling.

Looking back, however, I now see that God in His infinite wisdom and loving kindness knew exactly what He was doing.

But there was something else at play in my resistance to God's assignment for my life. I not only thought myself unworthy of what God was calling me to do, but, in all honesty, I didn't want it! You may be shocked at my admission, and you would not be the first. A hush falls over the sanctuary in the Potter's House whenever I reveal this on a Sunday morning, and most have heard me mention it before.

I suspect their gasps result from holding a preconceived notion about pastors *wanting* to preach. I am not saying that it's wrong for someone to desire to be used by God. When I look back over the years of ministry that I have under my belt and see all the hell that I have suffered, however, I would be lying to you if I told you that I didn't come close to throwing in the towel on numerous occasions.

Make no mistake about it; I love and value *everything* God has done in my life, and everything He continues to do. Nonetheless, if the Lord had allowed me to see the future when He called me, giving me a prophetic eagle's-eye view of everything that would come my way, I would have continued running. I would have been terrified at what would be required of me in those crushing moments to come. My ongoing flight would have been my first response, because the magnitude of our destinies often confounds our current immaturity.

God Won't Let Go

Why in the world would God handpick a country boy from the hills of West Virginia to preach for Him when there were so many other candidates that, from my point of view, were better choices? Like Moses, I came up with every excuse: I couldn't speak in front of crowds. I didn't like being around so many people at once. I had a speech impediment. My past was too dirty. *What good ever came out of West Virginia?* Anything that came to mind, I threw it at God as if He would listen to me and say, "You know what? You're right! I got it wrong this time. I'll find someone else. Sorry about that, Thomas."

When I think about it now, however, I wonder how I could have ever been so crazy to presume that I would know more than the Husbandman that cultivated me! The Master took everything into account when He chose me. He considered my past—as ugly as it was— and everything I would do in the future. He saw all of my insecurities and proclivities. He knew precisely where and how I would commit not only sins of ignorance but also those when I would *knowingly* transgress against him. I did everything I could to talk Him out of it and disqualify myself from His will for my life. The more I protested, the more He affirmed His call to me. The more I ran, the faster He chased. The more I dodged His pull on my life, the more vehemently He pointed at me. The more I hid, the more His eye concentrated on me. God just wouldn't let it go!

I was nineteen years old, just walking into the prime of my life, and God interrupted everything I had planned. Starting my ministry, I was so young that other ministers and preachers called me the "Boy Pastor," which wasn't exactly what I had in mind. This was not the direction in which I wanted to travel. Plucked from the path I had set for my life, that of a young businessman and entrepreneur, I found myself in the Husbandman's basket and being carried away from everything familiar so that He could fulfill all that He had placed in me. But I just wanted a normal life, a better life than my parents worked so hard to provide for me and my siblings. And I couldn't imagine scraping by as a pastor to be in line with what their efforts had produced—let alone better.

But how can a grape say to the Husbandman, "I don't want to be used to make wine!"

How could the clay ever protest to the Potter about what it was made for?

How could the clay ever protest to the Potter about what it was made for?

No matter what you do, when the Master has chosen you, there is no escaping His hand. When His eye rests upon you in the midst of the fields of humanity, you will never be able to hide. You still have a choice—God is always just as gentle as He is persistent—but it may feel like you will never have peace until you surrender.

As I think back, I now realize that the only reason I didn't want what God had for me was that the alternative, for all my dreams of being an entrepreneur, was just as bleak. I didn't think there was anything else better for me. Like Israel, I was content with the grapes of mediocrity, unaware the empowering impact crushing would have on my life.

Purpose in the Pattern

My dilemma was nothing new. The children of Israel also found themselves chosen for something they didn't quite understand when all they wanted was to have a normal life. Just as I had been plucked by the Vintner for His winemaking process, the Hebrew people, enslaved in Egypt for generations, had been waiting on God to deliver them. From my vantage point, I see that the entire time they were in Egypt, they were merely growing. Then, upon their escape, God sends them through the Red Sea, where He drowns those who had oppressed His children.

After they have been plucked from the hands of their oppressors and passed through the Red Sea for washing, God brought them out to the wilderness and instructed Moses to build the first tabernacle that would be erected to God and for His use. God's instruction was not general but quite specific as He desired Moses to build it according to the pattern the Lord provided (Exod. 25:40). Now if there is a pattern, we must recognize that its fulfillment relies on the reality on which that pattern is based. In other words, God had something special in mind with this blueprint He provided for His house where His people would worship Him. Therefore, when we look at the pattern for Moses' tabernacle, also called the tent of meeting, we pay close attention to three distinct sections: the outer court, the inner court or holy place, and the Most Holy Place or Holy of Holies. It looked like this:

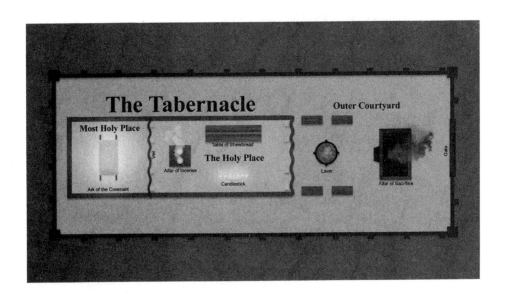

Anyone from the twelve tribes of Israel could enter the tabernacle's outer court to bring their sacrifices, but only priests could venture beyond that point. The access point to the tabernacle was on the eastern side, with only one entry point—one door, one gate (called the gate of the court)—through which anyone could gain entrance. God always allows everyone to have access to Him, and it was no different in the design of the tabernacle where He would dwell.

God always allows everyone to have access to Him, and it was no different in the design of the tabernacle where He would dwell.

Although basically anyone and everyone could enter this holy place, after gaining entrance to the outer court, however, *every* worshiper was expected to make a sacrifice. Simply put, God is holy and perfect, and human beings are sinful and imperfect. We cannot approach God without having some way to atone for our sins and experience His holy power. At this time, before the sacrifice of Jesus, the Lamb of God, people would bring an animal, usually an unblemished lamb, to offer God.

No way could this expectation to make a sacrifice slip anyone's mind because the largest piece of furniture in the entire tabernacle would quickly remind them of it. Standing there before them, just after the entrance, with a roaring fire emanating from it, was the brazen altar. This dramatic altar demanded a sacrifice, and anyone who desired an audience with God could not come empty-handed. The priests met every individual from the very moment they entered the tabernacle and collected the sacrifices and placed them on the altar to be burned.

Several steps away was another piece of furniture called the brazen laver, a basin made from the brass of the looking glasses, or mirrors, used by the women of the children of Israel. This basin would hold the water the priests would use to wash themselves before they proceeded farther into the tabernacle, after sacrifices were made. The temple priests had to purify themselves in order to receive sacrifices on behalf of God and to impart His forgiveness and blessing on His people. But these two key features of the brazen laver, mirrors and water, were not just for the priests of the tabernacle. They also symbolize the self-examination and cleansing required as we answer God's call and come before Him.

Reflecting and Cleansing

Without going into an extensive study of the entire tabernacle, which requires a book of its own, we find too many similarities to winemaking here in the outer court than I can resist. You see, the first thing God did with the children of Israel after they left Egypt was rid them of what had enslaved them by drowning the Egyptians in the Red Sea. In effect, God was cleansing Israel of all that had stained them for so long. He had already saved Israel from death by allowing an innocent animal to take the place of every person who decided to come up under His protection and enter into covenant with him. The marking set them apart from the Egyptians, who suffered death without the sacrificial blood to cover them, and protected each Hebrew household.

The crushing of the innocent animal came first. Covered in blood, as it were, they fled into the wilderness with Pharaoh's army in hot pursuit. Then when Israel reached the Red Sea, God opened a path through walls of water that towered above them on each side. Israel passed through the water and arrived safely on the other side, but the Egyptians who chased them did not.

Why one and not the other, we might wonder.

The Egyptians weren't in covenant with God, never having slain a lamb to be in that covenant and never having recognized the Almighty as the one and only God. Had they done all three of those and turned to God in repentance, I suspect the outcome would have been completely different. But more important, Israel survived because they *were* in covenant with God, and having been covered in the blood of the innocent lambs that were slain on their behalf, they entered into the largest baptism ever known.

In effect, the Red Sea served as the largest brazen laver in Israel's history. So what we have is a crushing that came first through the lamb, then a self-examination via the mirror of the Red Sea that showed Israel it cannot do without God, coupled with a washing that prepared Israel to meet God in the wilderness. In this progression of three events, we have the first three steps that take place at the tabernacle *and* the first three steps in the winemaking process.

The first thing to happen to grapes before they are crushed is that they are plucked from the vineyard and brought to the winepress. Once in the press, the heavy feet of the Husbandman and those facilitating the process would begin to trample upon the grapes, expressing from them the precious juice encased inside the fruit. In order for the juice to be extracted, however, the flesh of the fruit had to be crushed. For the grape to become what it really is, pressure had to be exerted. That same juice from the fruit would flow into a separate vat that would hold the fluid, but not before passing through a filter that would strain, or wash, the liquid and remove from it any additional pulp.

For the grape to become what it really is, pressure had to be exerted.

Right on the heels of crushing the grapes, there is a self-examination via the filter that leaves the Husbandman with a washed product He will use to make wine. This crushing coincides with the initial sacrifice that takes place right when the Israelites would enter the tent of meeting. Their sacrifice would be placed upon the brazen altar for the judgment of their sin. Instead of them being burned up, the animal would take their place. Just moments later, the priests would examine and wash themselves before they entered the holy place, or inner court.

Notice the pattern repeating itself? In each case,

crushing came first. Although we might not like it, the Husbandman is telling us that the same thing will happen to each individual that would approach Him through the door that is Christ our King. Right when we pass through the outer court gate, the first thing that all of us should expect is the sacrifice of pain that comes from the casting of our flesh onto the brazen altar that is the winepress of our Husbandman.

You cannot get around this crushing.

You cannot ignore it.

You must accept it.

Agony upon Entry

My own crushing did not end during the painful transition when I accepted God's call into full-time ministry. Thankfully, the passion I have for people lies at the center of my vocation and calling in the Kingdom because you cannot be a pastor and lead those you do not love. As an added benefit, I get to teach people about the Lord and who He is and what He does. I cannot fully explain to you the exuberance I experience upon seeing people filled with the love and righteousness of the Creator. As a result, leading people to Christ is not only my most pertinent assignment; it's also one of my greatest joys.

But I'm often taken aback by something—something that I see time and time again. Over the years, I've been labeled a "prosperity preacher" and myriad other titles that don't quite sum up the message of the gospel I deliver to others on a weekly basis. Please don't misunderstand me. I'm all for seeing people prospering in their lives, but that is not the root of the teachings that I minister. I stand solely on the redeeming blood of Christ, and it is the good news of our reconnection back to God as a result of Christ's finished work that I preach.

If you follow my teachings for a time, you will discover an ever-present characteristic that is pervasive throughout just about all my messages. I speak of *suffering*. I don't remove this subject from my sermons because our Vintner and True Vine experienced the worst suffering known to man, and he did it for a humanity that is quick to lean to their own understanding and flesh. I'm not a "Name-It-and-Claim-It," "Blab-It-and-Grab It," or "Five-Ways-to-Own-a-Bentley" type of pastor. So I marvel at the people who wrongfully believe that the acceptance of Christ into their lives equates to the absence of pain.

In fact, the opposite is true if we look in God's

Word. How can we be exempt from pain and trouble in the world when Jesus told us to expect the exact opposite? "I have told you these things, so that in me you may have peace. In this world you will have trouble. But take heart! I have overcome the world" (John 16:33).

When we look at the Old Testament and compare it to Christ's life, the first thing anyone should expect as they enter into a relationship with God is *trouble*. After all, it costs something to be unique. It costs something to be peculiar. It costs something to succeed. It costs something to produce quality. It even costs you something to be *you*!

Where in all the Word of God have we ever seen someone be blessed that did not, at first, go through tremendous pain? There is not a single gifted person that I know who cannot point to a tremendous amount of pain that fuels their giftings. The Bible is filled with examples of the downtrodden, the down-and-out, the forlorn and forgotten, and the powerless and poor being elevated and blessed in sight of society's elite. Those blessed people who seem to have come from nowhere didn't just get there for free. They paid dearly for what God gave them, and their currency was the tears that soaked their pillows at night and the blood issued from the wounds of their souls.

There is not a single gifted person that I know who cannot point to a tremendous amount of pain that fuels their giftings.

Agony is payable upon entry.

Just like we find with Israel's slavery in Egypt and their latter experience of the blessing of freedom in the wilderness, we see this same crushing upon entry to the tabernacle. Their sacrifice is the first thing handled, literally, right out the gate. So when it comes to our experiences as followers of Christ, why are we so befuddled when we encounter pain and stress in our lives? Jesus told us, "The kingdom of heaven is like a merchant seeking beautiful pearls, who, when he had found one pearl of great price, went and sold all that he had and bought it" (Matt. 13:45–46 NKJV).

Do you want to be all God created you to be? Do you want to fulfill your divine potential and enjoy the peace, purpose, and passion that come from the satisfaction of knowing your life has eternal significance? I suspect we would all answer that question affirmatively. We can pursue meaning, purpose, and pleasure in many ways but none satisfy in any lasting way like fulfilling the destiny God has for you.

So if this is truly what you want—which Jesus

compares to a precious, priceless pearl—then what are you willing to pay for it?

I cannot help but point out that Jesus chooses a pearl here and not another precious stone or valuable object. Do you know how pearls are formed? Pearls come from oysters or other shellfish like mussels and clams, and if these shelled creatures enjoy a calm, peaceful, pain-free existence, they never produce a pearl at all. They only create pearls if an irritant, like a tiny speck of pebble or sand or a parasite becomes trapped in the sensitive tissues within their hard shells. In order to soothe and remediate the pain caused by this invasive abrasion, oysters and shellfish emit a substance called nacre that coats the irritating invader with a smooth, slippery, translucent layer. They then repeat this process over and over until the irritant is coated with many layers of nacre, forming a beautiful pearl.

A pearl of great price is our pain wrapped in God's perfection.

A pearl of great price is our pain wrapped in God's perfection.

So please allow me to ask you again: Are you willing to pay the price for your pearl of great price?

God Shouts in Our Pain

Please do not misunderstand what I'm saying. Do I like pain? No healthy person enjoys the violation of excruciating discomfort, either acutely or chronically, that signals some problem or malfunction in our bodies and minds—not in the least bit. On the other hand, then, we might ask whether God enjoys sending us through pain. Hardly! God is not a sadist, and neither am I. But there is something we learn through the experience of pain and struggle that we don't learn anywhere else, and that is appreciation. For you do not love that which costs you nothing. And God paid the most expensive price in sending his Son for us.

God as our Husbandman beckons us to His winepress so that we may experience just a microscopic aspect of that pain in order that we would not only appreciate the blessings He gives us while on the planet, but also appreciate all the more what He did for us and the person into which He transformed us. It's as if the Vintner uses our pain, turmoil, and struggles as a tool of refinement. The great writer and Christian apologist C. S. Lewis said, "We can ignore even pleasure. But pain insists upon being attended to. God whispers to us in our pleasures, speaks in our conscience, but shouts in our pains: it is his megaphone to rouse a deaf world."

Blood is the price we pay for access to God, and it comes at great expense. Thankfully, Christ paid that price for us. Therefore, the sacrificial entrance fee for the tabernacle is represented by our Lord who was crushed on our behalf. From Israel's crushing in Egypt, to the crushing sacrifice at the brazen altar at Moses' tabernacle, to Christ's crushing by death on the cross, God has invited us to His winepress so that He can do with us that which is necessary to reconnect something temporal to its eternal source.

So please don't be surprised and begin to despair at the onset of the crushing you will endure. Don't run *from* it; run *to* it, because you're not being crushed simply for crushing's sake. God is getting this ugliness out of the way first, because the Shekinah Glory of the Lord is just two sections away from where you're standing now. James tells us, "Consider it pure joy, my brothers and sisters, whenever you face trials of many kinds, because you know that the testing of your faith produces perseverance. Let perseverance finish its work so that you may be mature and complete, not lacking anything" (James 1:2–4). Your pain is not going to last and, like the labor pains of an expectant mother, will produce new life.

Don't run from it; run to it, because you're not being crushed simply for crushing's sake.

Do you wish a connection and audience with God or not? Do you want more from life than you can ever experience on your own? If you do, you must embrace this aspect of the process, because the crushing is meant to do two things: get out of you what's in you, and get the true you out of the thin skin that encases you.

The crushing of the grape not only expresses the juice from the flesh, but it also separates the unusable parts of the grape from the juice. You see, it's one thing to be saved by Christ. Jesus handled your salvation at the brazen altar. It's another thing altogether to be sanctified by Christ and for His service. Just as the Israelites once stood at the brazen laver, you experience how the Lord not only saves you from what you did but also reveals the true you to yourself when you begin looking into the mirror of His perfect law of liberty.

After all, why save you from what your sin has made you and ignore showing you who and what you really are in Him? And the more you return to the mirror of God's Word, the more He reveals Himself in you, causing you to align with your true identity in Him. Crushing requires purification. Do you know anyone who would purify something they do not intend to use? Filth remains with refuse, but you clean that which is profitable and useful. As a result, your crushing cannot be the end, because God would never purify you if He didn't intend to use you.

Your crushing is nothing more than the beginning of a glorious transformation process that will reveal to the world and you who and what you really are. And it's just the first step. Just like the sacrifice at the tabernacle comes first, so does your crushing. Just like Israel's slavery came first, so does your crushing. Just like Moses' tabernacle was the first of the three mentioned in the Old Testament, your crushing is the first of three stages. Just like your acceptance of Jesus' death comes first, so does your crushing. Just like the grapes being trampled comes first, so does your crushing. There is more to come—so much more.

CHAPTER 7

Let's Make Wine

No one thinks of how much blood it costs.

—Dante

This is the end—you will lose it all!"

There we were, living in a big house and driving a nice car, but living paycheck to paycheck—and barely surviving. Even as my ministry was growing, the enemy kept whispering in my ear every night, "This is the end. You will never make it. You're about to lose everything!"

The cold heat of fear enters your heart when such words convey their message of imminent disaster. When your life begins to hemorrhage all that you hold dear, you know the reality of the fist clenching inside your gut could easily squeeze the life out of you. Such fear is particularly acute when you've been poor before, when you've had nothing and worked hard to attain your present level, precarious as it might be. I know what it's like to have utilities turned off and to be on food stamps and WIC. My family and I survived those times, but the very *smell* of it still terrified me.

The only difference between the time Serita and I were poor and this time was that we were wearing nicer clothes, living in a bigger home, and traveling more comfortably. As challenges mounted, I had to make the difficult choice between continuing to fight through the turmoil and endure it all, or throw in the towel and give up on the future God promised me. Even still, bankruptcy was knocking at my door every single day. Added to the weight of all this, I knew the responsibility of being the sole breadwinner for my entire family. I had a wife and five children to feed, and both of my siblings worked for me.

If that weren't enough, my growing church desperately needed a new facility. I was preaching five services every Sunday to a packed crowd and an overflow area at capacity. We needed more space yesterday. We had been denied a loan to build a larger church five times. Everywhere I ventured, I was told that I couldn't build what God had placed on my heart. I understood being denied the loan, but I could not stomach a stranger telling me that my mission was invalid and my vision was false.

The pressure to continue with all God called me to do.

The weight of providing for my family.

The bleeding of a leader who suffered in silence.

The crushing of my heart as I cried out to God.

You feel me? I'm talking about the pain you endure with tight lips, a straight back, and a head held high as you say to yourself the same prayer-like mantra uttered by Job thousands of years ago: "Though He slay me, yet will I trust Him" (Job 13:15 NKJV). So I continued even while everything around me was being crushed. I was back to standing and staring out the window on countless nights while searching for an answer and begging God with the words, "Lord, please get me out of this!"

Crushed for His Purpose

I didn't know that I was being crushed, that I was in a process ordained by the Master, that there was a purpose behind it all. The pressure God was applying to me was forcing my blood, sweat, and tears into the vision He had given me in order to give life to

143

my future. Coming from a family of entrepreneurs, I knew that nothing in my life would simply be handed to me. But it became all too apparent that I was not going to receive all that God had for me without a fight.

The enemy had showed his fangs and sharpened his claws in preparation to do me in. He saw my vulnerable state and tried to create an avalanche of turmoil to trip me, turn me, and torture me away from what I knew was my divine destiny. Although I knew about such obstacles from a cognitive, theological perspective, the reality left me battered, bruised, and bloody. And I know my experience reflects what we all face in some way.

In this crushing process, the enemy of your soul will send obstacles your way in order to convince you to abandon what God is doing in your life. Things you could not imagine will spring out of nowhere. People you thought you knew will disappoint you, fail you, betray you. Circumstances and events that seem to have no rhyme or reason will suddenly become the poetry you are forced to recite each day as the script of your life. I've been in the ministry for over forty years, and you'd be shocked at the problems and pressures that tried to run me off and sentence me to a life of mediocrity.

In this crushing process, the enemy of your soul will send obstacles your way in order to convince you to abandon what God is doing in your life.

During that time, I frequently sampled the bitterness of the bile that rose in my mouth, and it seemed as if it was the only comfort I had. I had to get up in the morning and smile and keep moving. I had to look okay while everything connected to me was collapsing. I was so worried that I couldn't even eat. I would only get about an hour or two of sleep and return to my misery of worry. Those are the nights that try men's souls.

"Get ready! Get ready! Get ready!"

I would preach those words on Sunday mornings to crowds of tens of thousands of people while I wrestled with the fact that I didn't know what I was getting ready for. I was ready for the ministry, the church, the press, and the IRS, but I was never ready for the crushings that would happen in my life. When you watch the broadcast and hear me teach and speak, you would never think I would be up at night, riddled with fear, frustration, and fright.

But, while you were up at three in the morning,

pacing in your house, I was stirring around in mine. The sermon that I preached to you the following Sunday was the one the Master personally ministered to me on Thursday night. You were never alone as you were being crushed. As we worried together about how the Master would get glory out of the painful moments of our lives, God was there, ensuring that the blood we were shedding would make it into the wine he would serve to others as a testament and promise that he can bring beauty and joy out of the ugliest and most depressing seasons of life.

The horrible parts of my bruisings were covered by my shoes. Every bit of success that I've had is sprinkled with the blood of the injuries that came from me being trampled under the feet of the Master. That evidence is in every accomplishment that I've ever gotten. My size 13 feet that went to the White House or walked across a stage so that I could receive a Grammy—those feet were always bruised and bloody, even though they were covered with polished leather shoes and dress socks. Before you follow anybody and allow them to pour into you, ask them to show you their soles. Because you cannot be a Savior or a successful person and not have bloody feet.

---

*You cannot be a Savior or a successful person and
not have bloody feet.*

Cost-Efficiency

Recently I wrote a book, aptly named *Soar!*, on using
one's entrepreneurial gifts to take flight and reach
new heights. Upon its release—in fact, even before
the book ever took shape—the questions I got asked
most frequently, usually by burgeoning entrepreneurs
and individuals inspired to launch a startup, were the
same:

> *Is the price worth the pain?*
> *What's the sum total that my transformation is going
>   to cost me?*
> *What will I have to give up in order to be what God
>   has inspired me to become?*

Whenever they pose such questions, my mind
recalls the late, great Kathryn Kuhlman, an amazing female evangelist before female evangelists were
widely accepted. She was dramatic in her delivery of
the Word and extremely effective. During one of her

sermons, she spoke about how much it cost her to be who she was. Her answer is the same one I offer to those who seek my business counsel. It is the same answer I now have for you: "It costs *everything*. If you really want to know the price, I'll tell you. It'll cost you everything."

This process is going to cost you what you know about yourself and all that is stable and familiar. It's going to cost you *everything*, and yet the Master is behind all of it, requiring that you ascertain whether you fully trust Him or not. In this process of crushing, God is switching you from the food of failure to the breakfast of champions. He's shifting the paradigm of your seed-like mentality of simply producing fruit into the glorious crushing of making wine. The problem with which we all must grapple is whether or not we are willing to pay the price for such a radical shift. And this shift takes time.

God is switching you from the food of failure to the breakfast of champions.

The process of developing excellence is never microwaved, and the transformation in which God has us requires staying power. Are you willing to stay in the midst of the pain? Are you willing to sacrifice the time it takes to be your best? Will you sacrifice what is good in your life in order to achieve the greatness latent within you?

The change and transformation we're enduring is a test of time. If we continue with the Master, the end result legitimizes the trauma of our pasts. If you don't bear the fruit of continuance, I become suspicious of the root of your conversion. In other words, you can tell how real God's process is in your life by whether you continue with Him. After all, you can only fake your desire for transformation for so long. That's why it requires faith—confidence in what cannot be seen by our mortal eyes and hope in the supernatural power of God to do the impossible in your life.

Change is a savage business, and you will easily part with its end results if you forget what it cost you. Yet with such a high price being required of us by the Master, who has an expected end for us, how could we ever forget that the wine He is producing in us is well worth it? Can we believe that the price we're paying as we water our seeds of greatness with our blood, sweat, and tears is truly worth it?

Body and Blood

In order to assess such cost-efficiency for our crushing, I ask you to join me as we eavesdrop on the Last Supper, the final meal Jesus had with His disciples prior to His death on the cross. There He is, the Master and Messiah, going to the upper room that had been selected and prepared, knowing He was about to cause His followers a major paradigm shift.

The time of year for this meal, remembering and celebrating the Passover, was no coincidence. Drinking and eating the Passover meal was a memorial to all the tragedy, terror, and travails the people of Israel endured in order to secure their freedom and eventually reach the Promised Land. The meal recognized being spared a visit by the Angel of Death by the blood of the lamb smeared on each Hebrew doorpost. The annual event celebrated Moses leading them through the Red Sea only to watch the walls of water crash down behind them on Pharaoh's army in hot pursuit.

At this Passover meal, however, Jesus took the same elements that had been used for generations and completely transformed their meaning. Imagine the shock on the faces of His disciples as their Leader took the bread, broke it, and said, "Take and eat; this is my body" (Matt. 26:26). How could something made of wheat flour and water be the living flesh of Jesus' body? Even if the bread represented the sacrifice of the lamb back in Egypt, how could that lamb now become the Lamb of God?

Only later, looking back, would they realize that the Body of Christ—the broken bread—was being passed to the Body of Christ—the church and communion of saints—by the Body of Christ, Jesus, God's only Son, living on the earth as a man of flesh and blood. There in that moment at the Last Supper all reality, seen and unseen, visible and invisible, on heaven and on earth, collided in the crushing.

Then Jesus took the cup of wine—I'm told that at Passover there were usually four cups used to represent different aspects of the historical remembrance—and said, "Drink from it, all of you. This is the blood of the covenant, which is poured out for many for the forgiveness of sins" (Matt. 26:27–28). If the bread becoming the Body of Christ was a stretch, then the wine becoming the blood of Christ must have really blown their minds! After seeing Him walk on water, heal the sick, and raise the dead, with Him standing right there in their midst, what in the world was Jesus talking about? Bread and wine? Body and blood?

Certainly with wine and blood, there is a similarity in appearance if not consistency. But beyond the deep red color, for their Master to say that the fermented fruit of the vine was His actual blood, the blood that was about to be shed so that all sins could be forgiven—it was unimaginable. And yet, wine is indeed blood—the blood of the vine, the essence, the juice of the fruit crushed for its creation.

From Passover to that first communion, we find the tipping point of our salvation in that upper room. The price was about to be paid on the cross for the wine we continue to drink, just as we eat the bread, commemorating the broken body and bloodshed of our Lord. And it's no surprise—the price was everything.

God Pays the Price

There's not much you can do with grapes that will increase their value. There are only two worthwhile things you can do: nurture them with your hand or crush them under your feet for making wine. The Lord endured His own painful process to grow us into something that would become what He already is.

The Lord endured His own painful process to grow us into something that would become what He already is.

Christ is the person gathering the grapes of our lives, having to reach between our branches to obtain them and risk getting pricked and bruised by our thorns we use to protect ourselves. Simultaneously, He is the person who treads the grapes in the press, getting His feet scarred in the process. Looking at Christ, we should see that He is making wine out of us and His own bruised places because it's in the crushing vats that the wine of the grapes and the blood of His feet are mixed.

He's paying a personal cost for our transformation.

You might grasp a small understanding of your own pain in moments of crushing, but have you ever stopped to think about and appreciate what it costs God to see you through the process? The protection that's required to keep you safe, and the provision you need in order to keep growing and evolving? Parents understand the overwhelming sacrifice it costs to successfully develop a child into a healthy and mature adult.

I look at the thriving individuals my children have become and realize that they don't remember everything Serita and I had to go through for them to be who they are. I can't begin to tell you the trials and traumas we endured over the years of their formation. From interactions with neighbors to medical crises, from bullies to breakups, their mother and I have suffered in order for them to grow stronger.

As our children matured and became teenagers, we had to suffer their insults and restrain ourselves from issuing certain responses, lest we said or did something we could not take back. We had to sacrifice our plans in favor of those of our kids. There were times Serita and I went without in order to provide for our children, who at the time couldn't understand the cost. But we were willing to pay that price so we could make the wine that we now enjoy in each of their lives.

It's the same between God and you. For, whenever you are developing people, you bleed like a Messiah because you can't help others without getting stained feet and cut hands. It costs you something to make a difference in anyone's life. Why, then, would we think we're the only ones receiving and paying the invoices for our transition? After all, we entered into this transaction with insufficient funds, requiring the Master to do for us what we could not do for ourselves.

Profit from the Pain

No one can skirt around their involvement in and dedication to and wearing the evidence of the work it took in bringing something to birth. The juice of the grapes that you crush saturates your feet, but your feet are bruised as your unique footprint indelibly marks the fruit. The fruit and Vinedresser are marked by one another. If your hands and feet are scarred, isn't your DNA in the wine of the grapes you trampled? Until what you seek to change has your scent on it with your blood, sweat, and tears in it, are you really making a difference at all?

The fruit and Vinedresser are marked by one another.

We have plenty of people trying to change the nation, build a business, or begin some other enterprise, but they don't want anyone to see their feet for fear of being embarrassed by their bruises. Nevertheless, your battle scars are your personal testimony that tells me you've been crushed. It is impossible for me to see you as credible until I see the scars in your hands and your DNA in what you're offering. This is why it was necessary for Christ to be the first fruits and first barrel of wine that God introduced to humanity.

Likewise, it costs you something to be great—it costs you everything. Regardless of where you find yourself in life, you paid a price to be there. This sounds like a simple truth, but you would be surprised by the number of people who never consider what it costs to simply be themselves. Whether they are a CEO, spouse, parent, or teenager, something was given in exchange for them to be where they are and who they are. Either they footed the bill, or someone else chipped in. Regardless of your background, you will have to trade something of extreme value for you to become the person God has called you to be.

So what are you willing to barter in exchange for your future?

Keep in mind that being great is not classified only by financial gain or notoriety. Greatness is the level to which God takes you where you are finally operating with confidence and fullness in the environment he has placed you in. It's where you are being all you can be for His glory. But no one suddenly matriculates to greatness. It is developed in you over a period of time in which God transforms you level by level into who He has designed you to be. Like a seed, greatness lives inside you, but it must be cultivated as He guides you through the various seasons of change. And it's in the changes of life that the costliest transactions take place.

Like a seed, greatness lives inside you, but it must be cultivated as He guides you through the various seasons of change. And it's in the changes of life that the costliest transactions take place.

We have a mandate on our lives to seek profitability after the agony of our crushing. So let's revisit the question. Is the cost worth it? And allow me to answer by asking a different question: Is there any profit? Yes! Beyond compare, the cost of the wine is more than worth the suffering. Jesus endured the shame of the cross for the joy set before Him (Heb. 12:2). His joy blossomed in the church of the New Testament, His bride, which could not have existed any other way. Christ knew that His suffering, anguish, humiliation, pain, and shame were necessary.

He knew they were part of the cost in the Garden of Gethsemane when He prayed to His Father and asked that His cup—the cup of wine from the previous night that was now about to become the cup of His blood—might pass by Him (Matt. 26:36–46). We're told, "And being in anguish, He prayed more earnestly, and His sweat was like drops of blood falling to the ground" (Luke 22:44). Meanwhile, His disciples—those who were closest to Him and cared the most—had fallen asleep. Jesus suffered alone long before He died on the cross. Gethsemane was His place of crushing.

But oh, the sweetness of the wine our Lord was making! When you pay the price of crushing, the wine you make is beyond compare. Out of the bloodshed and bruising, rising up from the depths of fear and grief pulling you under, something is growing. You're being crushed right now, but there is something in you that will survive. Let's make wine!

You're being crushed right now, but there is something in you that will survive. Let's make wine!

Little did I know when I stood sweating in the Mississippi heat as a sixteen-year-old boy beside my father's grave that not only would I survive the devastating crushing of my soul, but I would also make new wine. Little could I imagine as I watched my car being repossessed that I would have more than enough wine for myself, my family, and others I'm allowed to bless. Little could I see how those sleepless nights would be more than worth the wine of meeting kings and presidents, ministering to millions of people around the world, and pastoring my flock.

My story is no different from what God is doing in your life.

For everything you've lost, for all that's been trampled, let's make wine.

For every scar on your body and every fracture in your heart, let's make wine.

For every lost relationship and broken promise, let's make wine.

For every stolen dollar and wasted opportunity, let's make wine.

For every tear shed and every pain suffered, God is at work in your life.

Let's make wine!

CHAPTER 8

Power in the Blood

The blood was shed to unite us to God.
—Andrew Murray

Making wine requires more than changing the way you see your life. Spiritually speaking, making wine requires bloodshed. The importance of blood throughout Scripture cannot be overestimated because, through it, we see that our position with God is changed. As a result, it makes sense that our identities would change, as well. We see this transformative process illustrated in numerous ways throughout the Bible, but one instance has always intrigued and disturbed me.

CRUSHING

The importance of blood throughout Scripture cannot be overestimated because, through it, we see that our position with God is changed.

At a lodging place on the way, the LORD met Moses and was about to kill him. But Zipporah took a flint knife, cut off her son's foreskin and touched Moses' feet with it. "Surely you are a bridegroom of blood to me," she said. So the LORD let him alone. (At that time she said "bridegroom of blood," referring to circumcision.) (Exod. 4:24–26)

Obviously, a lot of forces are converging in these three little verses. The context is seemingly simple: God has asked Moses to take his wife, Zipporah, and his children from Midian back to Egypt in order to confront Pharaoh and initiate the freedom of the people of Israel. Along the way, however, we have this little incident recounted here.

I can just imagine it. To compound matters, every ounce of the white-hot anger that coursed through Zipporah's veins was mixed with a dose of betrayal. She could hardly stomach how her life had been upended by Moses, but here she was, pacing in the middle of the night in the wilderness, trying to wrap her mind around remarkably strange orders that prompted her husband to go back to Egypt—the very nation in which he was declared a fugitive.

Moses slept just feet away from the fire that still bathed the immediate area in a warm glow of orange and yellow, shielding them against the sharp night winds of the desert that plummeted an average of thirty degrees. Next to him was their sleeping son. His slumber made him oblivious to his mother's rage-filled patrol and his father's snoring. Zipporah couldn't take it. She had to walk—do something—to take her mind off what had disrupted her life. All she had for company were the myriad stars that didn't leave a single vacancy in the night sky.

Moses' account of his conversation with *something* was absolutely mind-boggling, not to mention how his stuttering and stammering made his retelling of the farfetched tale even worse. A talking burning bush that didn't burn up? Moses had to have been out with the sheep for entirely too long. The heat must have gotten to him. There was absolutely no other rationale that could explain such insane behavior, and for her father to grant Moses permission to return to Egypt served only to further incense Zipporah.

Surely, something had to give, but Moses was her husband. Divorce was completely out of the question, and she could not abandon him. She was tied to the man, being in love with Moses from the first moment she laid eyes on him. When she met him, she dismissed Moses' Egyptian garb as mere remnants of where he came from. "He must have grown tired of his native land," she reasoned to herself. Their love was rapturous, and Moses took to shepherding sheep quite well, almost as if he was born to lead and care for things so innocent. His speech was something people laughed at, but Zipporah thought the impediment an attractive quirk that made Moses even more alluring. "It's rather cute," she affectionately shot at him as she passed by him one day.

Glances turned to flirts. Flirts gave way to in-depth conversations. Conversations transformed into endless moments of hanging around one another. Jethro, the high priest of Midian, observed it all and was satisfied with their fondness for each other that never crossed the line. Moses was honorable, and Jethro even perceived how Moses took pride in his work around the village, noticing Moses' happiness with his lot in life and his growing affinity for his daughter. The runaway Egyptian-turned-shepherd wasn't the first choice he had for his Zipporah, but he knew he couldn't stand in the way of such an organic relationship. It was only logical to marry them.

All was well until Moses' encounter with the Most High.

Under Your Skin

Being the Midian high priest, Jethro possessed a discernment that instantly confirmed the truth of Moses' account of what happened while he tended the flocks so many weeks ago. There was an urgency in Moses' speech and eyes that he had never witnessed before. The lad's easygoing demeanor was nowhere to be found, and he could barely get his words out. Surely, Moses had seen *something*, and far too many people knew Jethro was not to be trifled with when it came to dealing with issues he believed were divine.

Still, Zipporah was beyond incensed. The way she saw her life was completely destroyed. No more would Moses arrive at their home in the evening and dust off his feet from having shepherded the sheep. No more would there be simple days that ended with Zipporah locked in the arms of her husband, content with the unaltered schedule they lived each day. This new God Moses spoke of did a number on him, and Zipporah was forced to acquiesce to a deity she had never worshiped. Having heard of the litany of gods in Egyptian lore, she had never heard of one who so audaciously referred to itself as "I Am."

Whoever he was, he had gotten Moses' attention, and Zipporah didn't like it. There were customs that Moses spoke of, strange traditions that he said his people had been following for generations even while in captivity. One stood out the most to Zipporah, and that's where she immediately drew the line. There was no way she would allow Moses to take a knife to their son's penis and remove his foreskin.

"You are absolutely out of your mind!" Zipporah fumed when Moses approached her with the thought. "I've been beyond patient with you and all of this, even to the point of leaving my home for you and this... *quest*. I will *not* put my son through that kind of pain. Why in the world do you think I would allow you to do that to *our* boy—*our son*? No! This far, no further!"

She remembered Moses' anger and frustration burning like fire in his eyes. It was all he could do to not force the issue. She had thrown down the gauntlet. Zipporah left Moses with the choice between the traditions of his heritage that, up until a few months ago, she could have sworn was Egyptian, and choosing his family. Everything in her was shaken to the core, but Zipporah couldn't handle another change, not one so massive that would physically affect their child in such a way. More than the relief she experienced when Moses wrapped his arms around her in surrender to her demands, Zipporah's rattled soul was soothed by the thought that there were some things Moses would refuse to do even in the face of this new God she had heard nothing about.

But now she was about to lose him—and their son. Standing near her husband and son, she saw Moses unconsciously fighting for his life and battling convulsions that rattled his entire body. She saw no reason for the violent seizure, no prints or marks in the sand that led her to believe an animal or insect had caused Moses' condition. Their son, oddly, was still in the deepest of sleep, almost comatose.

Moses shuddered uncontrollably as Zipporah knelt beside him, trying her best to rouse him from his sleep. "Moses! Moses, my love, wake up! *MOSES!*" A profuse, unending sweat soaked through Moses' clothes and skin as if he were being submerged in a bath. His breathing immediately went from labored to raspy to nonexistent. Zipporah released a blood-curdling scream of Moses' name that failed to wake her husband and her son.

Zipporah, holding Moses' head in her hands, searched her immediate area for a handle on the moment. Tears flooded her eyes and streamed down her face. Her husband was dying, and there was nothing she could do about it. Her anger and resentment toward him had completely disappeared and been replaced by sheer panic at the thought of losing him. There was no time for prayer, only action. And to which being would she pray? The gods of her fathers? Moses' God? If there was anyone that would stop Moses from dying, surely it would be the One who sent him on this mission in the first place, correct? Why would he order Moses to a task that he could never complete? And, how could she even contact him?

Zipporah was on her feet in a flash and looking through a pack that sat atop a nearby camel. Searching through it and not finding a knife, she spotted a nearby sharp stone. She picked it up and dashed back to her son. Standing over the boy, she was gripped with fear as to whether or not her harm of him would work. But, there was too much to lose—too much at stake. Zipporah, completely unsure of herself, dropped to her knees beside her son and kissed his face, thanking whatever God that was listening that her son was still asleep. She could get the worst of the emergency surgery out of the way before the boy knew what hit him.

Zipporah removed her son's pants, exposing his genitals to the night air, and cut into his foreskin. The boy's cries were deafening, but Zipporah was already halfway done and pushed through his agony to the end.

"I'll be right back, my son."

Having removed the extra flesh from him, Zipporah crawled to Moses while cradling the bloody knife and extra skin of her son. She smeared her son's blood on her husband's feet. Her voice trembled as she uttered, "Surely you are bridegroom of blood to me."

Moses inhaled a gigantic breath, the sound of which almost eclipsed his son's screams. Color returned to his skin, becoming the human hue of red as his cells began receiving oxygen. Zipporah cradled her husband's head in her arms as his eyes burst open and he attempted to sit up. Just as quickly as Moses became deathly ill, the ordeal ended after Zipporah applied the circumcision blood.

Moses, recognizing what happened, hugged Zipporah before he and his wife saw to their son's injury.

Cutting a New Name

Forgive me for dramatizing this bizarre surgery in the ancient desert on the edges of Egypt, but it demands not just our understanding but our experiential appreciation. Just about any man would be hesitant to line up for a circumcision at a mature age.

Simply put, being approached with a knife is already something that would give anyone pause. However, someone approaching you with a knife for circumcision might cause them some injury. We all have our limits, and I believe each man of age would consider that as one of them. Yet, God approached Moses that evening for the very thing that was required of every Hebrew male on the eighth day of his life. But, looking within Exodus 4:18–31, it's quite clear that Moses had not led his son under the knife.

I must admit that this is a peculiar passage in the Bible, and one that troubled me for many years. I wrestled back and forth with the question of why an omniscient, omnipresent, and omnipotent God would commission Moses to carry out His orders of setting His people free and, while he was on his way to do just that, suddenly decide to kill him. Why would God go back on His word? Was circumcision that serious? If so, why?

It was the humanity in me that was asking such questions. However, God's divinity spoke, and I realized that if God really wanted Moses dead, Zipporah could have done nothing to stop it. It's quite possible, then, that God did not require Moses' life, as some have been led to believe. Rather, God was proving a point that would be illustrated over and over again throughout Scripture. If circumcision was so important to God that His visit almost killed Moses, doesn't that warrant us looking back at its institution? It's that question that directed me back to Abram. Notice that I spoke of his old name (Abram) and not the one he was later given by God (Abraham).

It's in Genesis 17 that we first hear about circumcision, and though the very thought of it frightens most men to their core, it was something that Abram did to *himself* not at eighteen, thirty, or even sixty years of age. Abram performed his own circumcision at the tender old age of ninety-nine! It's here that an overwhelming population of sensical people begin shouting their question: *Who would do such a thing, and why?* Well, I offer nothing better than God's own words:

When Abram was ninety-nine years old, the LORD appeared to him and said, "I am God Almighty; walk before me faithfully and be blameless.

Then I will make my covenant between me and you and will greatly increase your numbers."

Abram fell facedown, and God said to him, "As for Me, this is my covenant with you:

You will be the father of many nations. No longer will you be called Abram;

your name will be Abraham, for I have made you a father of many nations.

I will make you very fruitful; I will make nations of you, and kings will come from you.

I will establish my covenant as an everlasting covenant between me and you and your descendants after you for the generations to come, to be your God and the God of your descendants after you.

The whole land of Canaan, where you now reside as a foreigner,

I will give as an everlasting possession to you and your descendants after you; and I will be their God."

Then God said to Abraham, "As for you, you must keep my covenant, you and your descendants after you for the generations to come. This is my covenant with you and your descendants after you, the covenant you are to keep:

Every male among you shall be circumcised. You are to undergo circumcision, and it will be the sign of the covenant between me and you.

For the generations to come every male among you who is eight days old must be circumcised, including those born in your household or bought with money from a foreigner—those who are not your offspring.

Whether born in your household or bought with your money, they must be circumcised.

My covenant in your flesh is to be an everlasting covenant. Any uncircumcised male, who has not been circumcised in the flesh, will be cut off from his people; he has broken my covenant." (Gen. 17:1–14)

In establishing a new covenant with Abram, God's first order of business was changing Abram's identity. In the fifth verse, God moved Abram from one position to another by calling Abram to a different walk. Instead of pursuing his own path, Abram was to follow the path laid out for him by God, and that is precisely where many of us falter. We seek our own way, not understanding that our pride and arrogance lead us into destruction. We hate having to receive instructions from anyone because we think we have a handle on everything in our lives. As a result, we don't like relinquishing control and walking with God by faith.

In establishing a new covenant with Abram, God's first order of business was changing Abram's identity.

We often make the mistake of labeling people based on what they've done. However, in labeling someone by what they've done, wouldn't we always be forced to call someone by what they did last? God doesn't do the same thing with us. The Master always calls us by what he has placed in us and what we will do for him. I submit to you that God calls us what we will be while we're wrestling with what we were and what we did. When God changed Abram's name, He increased the distance between who the man once was and who God told him he would be in the future. To better understand that distance, all we must do is compare the names.

According to the text, *Abram* means "high/exalted father," while *Abraham* means "father of many nations." The covenant God initiated in Abram becoming Abraham points to something God has been doing with humanity for thousands of years. The Master continuously speaks the truth to mankind about who and what we are, and he confirms this new identity that we have through the shedding of blood. The sign of Abraham's new persona was that he was required to cut away the foreskin from his penis.

Other than the pain involved, this might seem insignificant until we take into account that the surrounding people in the land of Canaan didn't call for males to undergo the cutting until puberty or their entrance into marriage. Standing starkly in contrast to the people around him, Abraham was to not only circumcise every male in his house, but also perform the rite on the eighth day of life. Eight being the number of new beginnings, each male entered into a new relationship with God on that day, being marked as someone else and part of something exclusive to everyone in his lineage.

Not only did Abraham receive a new name that signified who he was in God's eyes, but he and every man and boy in his house—indentured servants included—bore the physical proof that they were not like the men of the surrounding countries and societies. So exhaustive and complete was God's promise to Abraham that it not only extended to every man and boy associated with Abraham, but also to his wife, Sarai, who God renamed as Sarah.

Through this point, you can see that God is not interested in just changing you and your life. He is complete, all-encompassing, consuming and filling everything and everyone that belongs to him. God does not only seek your mind, or your heart, or your body. The Master wants the totality of who and what you are because you will receive nothing less from him. As a result, Abraham could not be the only person that this new covenant would affect. Sarah had to be part of it because Sarah was one flesh with Abraham.

God's blessings become reality in our lives when we rejoin the Master's plan by lining up with it in faith, like Abraham. In essence, when we reconnect with God, we step into what He has for us.

When we reconnect with God, we step into what He has for us.

Connecting by Covenant

Before Abram became Abraham by entering into covenant with God, we cannot dispute the fact that he was just another Semite in Canaan. The moment he received his mandate and new name from God is the moment he and everyone attached to him became someone else. The same was true of Moses. Before he entered into the service and worship of God, he was nothing more than a man with a mistaken identity who was raised as another one of the hundreds of thousands of Egyptians. Not until the Lord appeared to Moses in the burning bush did he become something else. It's here that the reconnection of his entire house back to God via the circumcision of his son became intensely necessary. This is also where we see the similarity the enslaved Hebrews had with Abraham and Moses.

Spending an extensive amount of time with other people causes you to adopt mannerisms and customs that aren't indicative of how you were raised. Granted, there are things that are simply part of you, aspects of who you are that will never change no matter your environment. Nevertheless, you pick up habits you never thought you would possess. You use words, phrases, and languages that were once alien to you. You develop an affinity for cuisine that tastes nothing like the foods you grew up eating. What's attractive to you is completely different from what you considered normal in your past. Even entertainment is different. At first, minute details that mean nothing to the indigenous people stand out to you, but soon become customary parts of your daily life.

This happened with the Hebrews, yet one tradition was a constant.

For nearly half a millennium, the descendants of Israel were constantly being exposed to a culture that was completely contradictory to their own. As a result, it's not too far-fetched for us to believe that they lost touch with some of their cultural traditions. However, there was one thing that persisted:

circumcision. The timing and consistency of this ritual and covenant were the only things they all held to that differentiated them from their Egyptian overlords. Imagine, then, how it would look for Israel's deliverer to show up, proclaim the message of freedom to them and Pharaoh, be used by God to send ten utterly devastating plagues to the land, and not even be in complete compliance with the tradition that sets them apart.

Every aspect of Moses, from his own body to that of his seed, had to bear resemblance to the people he would be leading out of bondage. If his life didn't line up with what God said about his people, how could the Israelites trust a leader that didn't obey the One who began the covenant in the first place? No leader can lead anyone where they have not yet been.

The similarity between Abraham, Moses, and the Hebrew nation is that neither of them looked to be anything special when seen through the untrained eye. Neither man nor the entire group was cut off from God or each other. They remembered who they were, though they were in completely alien environments. Abraham was called away from the land of his fathers and became the friend of God by simply believing him. Moses, while in Midian, became the deliverer of the children of Israel because he accepted his calling on his life to venture back to Egypt. The

Israelites were nothing but slaves to the Egyptians, but in keeping their side of the covenant with God, they were constantly reminded that God would extricate them out of slavery and exact judgment on the people who dared touch his children.

If God kept His word to Abraham, Moses, and the entire nation of Israel because of them remaining in covenant and connected to Him, why in the world would you think He wouldn't keep his word to you?

Remember the fact we've already established: God is ardently and passionately obsessed with getting his family back together. He is a Master totally consumed with reconnecting his children back to Him. For, in that connection, there are promises and blessings the Lord wants us to enjoy because of us simply being in his family. The only thing we must do is be just as desperate for reconnection back to him as he is. And that reconnection calls for us to be in covenant with him via a circumcision that is no longer physical, but spiritual and of the heart.

God is ardently and passionately obsessed with getting his family back together.

The Saving Blood of a Son

As a father of five grown children, three of them grown men, I take extreme pride in my sons. Of course, I am overwhelmingly proud of my daughters as well. Nevertheless, there exists between fathers and sons a connection that cannot be quantified. Seeing smaller, spitting images of yourself running around is quite alarming, yet endearing. Part of you wants them to be like you, but maturity steps in and changes that desire into allowing them to become what God would have them to be. You want them to be the best they can be, doing everything you can for your sons to become better men than the man you are.

I always wondered what went through Moses' mind when his son was eight days old. Did he even think about circumcising him? Seeing that once Moses was weaned, he was raised in the upper echelons of Egypt, I would assume that he was an educated man. Just looking back at the advanced nature of the Egyptian culture, we see that the people possessed an extremely high level of intelligence. To this day, we are still finding, studying, and being baffled by the ruins of ancient Egypt. So, I cannot excuse Moses' lapse in completing the ritual with his son to something as simple as "he didn't know." For how can the people who raised you be in the midst of enslaving your brothers and sisters and you not know a single shred about the customs of their captives? *Someone*—even an Egyptian priest—had to know something about the religious practices of their slaves and, in mere passing, mentioned it to Moses.

Believe it or not, I asked all of these questions and more in an attempt to understand why Moses didn't use his knife on his own boy when the baby was only eight days old. The only two conclusions I arrived at that made sense to the degree that either would override Moses' knowledge of the procedure was the speculation that Zipporah didn't agree with it, or Moses wanted to distance himself from everything that was in Egypt after he became a murderer and escaped the country. This includes the customs of his own people.

Nevertheless, the question had to rear its head again when Moses finally follows God's command to return to Egypt and free his people. It's here that the answer regarding Zipporah's obstinacy and objection to circumcision makes the most sense. Even if Moses thought it wasn't necessary to do, or Zipporah disapproved, they certainly received the rudest of awakenings when God visited them on their return trip to Egypt.

I cannot agree with the thought that God was going to *kill* Moses. Yes, the Bible said that Moses would have died. However, had the Almighty sought Moses' life to kill him, who would have been able to stop him? I also must look at Genesis 22:11–12 and note the fact that God required Abraham to sacrifice his only son and, while Abraham was about to plunge the knife into his boy, God stopped him and pointed to the ram in the bush he had provided. God's stopping of Abraham's hand, along with his ability to kill Moses and not going through with it, leads me to believe that Moses' death was not the Master's objective.

If killing Moses wasn't what God was after, what was his goal? The first thing that jumped out at me was the detail we noted not too far back: Moses could not be an effective leader in bringing the children of Israel out of Egypt while he or his family members stood in stark disobedience to the traditions that the Israelites managed to honor even when under slavery. Being a totally free man, Moses couldn't have answered their questions regarding his lack of compliance with "Oh, I just haven't gotten around to it yet."

Then again, some people believe Moses was uncircumcised and God was after him for noncompliance. I don't believe that is the case, and there is one main reason why. However, there are schools of thought and scholars that believe Moses and other individuals who feature prominently within Hebrew history were born aposthic, or without their foreskin. In essence, some believe Moses and these other men were born circumcised. Within the pages of *Abot De-Rabbi Natan* (The fathers according to Rabbi Nathan) is a list of these men, which includes Adam, Seth, Noah, Shem, Jacob, Joseph, Moses, and others.

Our subscription to the thought about Moses' aposthia is unnecessary. In addition, Moses being circumcised or uncircumcised isn't the question, because the text begs us to view what happened with his son and see that there must be something more. I am not saying that the vagueness of whether or not Moses was circumcised is not of issue. I just cannot imagine Moses being out of covenant with the Lord and him having a relationship with Moses that was so intimate that God described it by saying: "With him I speak face to face, clearly and not in riddles" (Num. 12:8).

A relationship like that with the Almighty does not come without God bringing that person into covenant with him. Whether Moses was circumcised on the eighth day or born circumcised, as some scholars believe, isn't the subject at hand because clearly the Lord favored and called him. And there is no way that God would not justify the servant he has called.

A relationship like that with the Almighty does not come without God bringing that person into covenant with him.

So, again, what was God after in visiting Moses?

Early on in my relationship with God, I began noticing that he is a manifold Master, possessing *many folds* in his wisdom and ways. It's almost as if he loves to leave his signature on things in order to point you back to him. Seeing how I have noticed how consistently he has done this in my life, I cannot help but search for his unique signature in all of Scripture. This means me looking for the reality of his word in the flesh form, which is Christ.

That is when something quickly grabbed my attention. Jesus' name in Hebrew is *Yeshua*, and that name carries within its meaning words such as *salvation* and *protection*. What if God was showing us that there is more to circumcision than just keeping our side of an eternal bargain? What if God was giving us a preview of what Jesus would do for us when he finally arrived on earth and set about working in his ministry and sacrificing his life on our behalf? It only makes sense. After all, we can see that, though

Zipporah might have detested the practice, the circumcision and injury of their son saved his father's life!

In other words, there is protection in circumcision! But, protection from *what*?

Signed in Blood

The answer to that question is quite simple: separation from God, which is death! We are inundated with myriad examples of how blood acts as a covering to those who enter into covenant with God. We see this truth first borne out in the Garden of Eden in Genesis 3:21 when God takes the life of an innocent animal and uses its skin to cover Adam and Eve's nakedness. In Genesis 4:4-5, you'll see that Abel brought to the Lord an acceptable sacrifice that consisted of fat portions from the firstborn of his flock. *Keep in mind that it was from the firstborn.* Later, when Moses gives instructions about the Passover in Exodus 12:1-13, he commands the children of Israel to take a *lamb without defect*, eat it, and place its blood on the doorframes of each house.

Do you see God's signature pointing back to Christ? There is something about the power of blood that God wants us to see! Our transformation into wine requires that we be signed and sealed by blood.

Our transformation into wine requires that we be signed and sealed by blood.

Just like the firstborn of Abel's flock; the lamb without defect at the first Passover; and the innocent animal God used to cover Adam and Eve's nakedness, God is continuously pointing us toward the future actions of Christ on our behalf. When it comes to the covering of our nakedness and shame, Jesus is the innocent life taken in the Garden of Eden to cover over the multitude of our sins. Christ is the perfect, unblemished firstborn of Abel's flock that serves as our identification, representing all of us before a holy and righteous King. At the Passover, Jesus is the spotless lamb that was killed and whose blood is sprinkled on the doorposts of our hearts, thereby sparing us when the Angel of Death came calling for justice.

In each of these examples, something else dies instead of the human being involved in the situation. Were Adam and Eve innocent? Hardly not. They were expelled from the Garden and, later, died because of their actions. And, we'll die, too. If Abel skipped out on giving God his best, would He have been seen as having done what was right? Not at all. Even more, what would have happened to the remainder of his flock? Simply look at the actions of his brother, Cain, and God's words to him for further proof.

Were the children of Israel without sin? Assuredly not, because they were fallible human beings with Moses, himself, being a murderer! The shedding of the blood of each of the animals involved, particularly the lamb at Passover, wasn't because the people in either situation were innocent. No, as representation or substitution, the blood of each animal was to show that death, in some form, had already been to the house and that it need not revisit.

Now considering all that we've explored, let's reconsider Moses and Zipporah on the way back to Egypt. At that time, his son wasn't circumcised. Moses' son being outside of covenant with God meant that some aspect of Moses and his family was exposed to a considerable amount of danger. Moses, being the emissary of God sent to Pharaoh, needed to be covered on every side of his life. Anything left to chance could have been exploited to force Moses out of his mission. Seeing that he was not walking around with physical bodyguards and security forces that could effectively handle Egyptian soldiers, what better way to get Moses to step away from calling down plagues upon Egypt than to hold his son hostage?

Before Moses' enemies in Egypt could take advantage of such an opportunity, God exposed the chink in the armor and showed us modern-day and contemporary believers what Christ did for us. Where we saw a foretaste of Jesus' actions in the Garden with Abel and what would happen at the Passover, a picture of Jesus is shown to us through Moses' boy.

Moses' son, because of uncircumcision, had no identity or part with the everlasting covenant God established with the Hebrew people. He was on his own. He had no entitlement to anything Moses would bequeath to him. He had no access to protection. The Law given later would have prevented him from taking part in the Passover meal that commemorates the freeing of his extended family. In essence, the boy could have been considered illegitimate—a bastard, if you will—just like we were before encountering and surrendering ourselves to Christ.

Then, God visited Moses. Zipporah, desperate to save her husband, casts aside her own distaste toward the ritual and capitulates to God's demands that any and all of his children reconnect back to him via covenant. Zipporah takes a sharp stone, performs the surgery and, according to the Bible, touches Moses' member with it. Moses' very life is saved at the exact moment the blood of his *firstborn son*—now in covenant—touches him. In other words, Moses' error in not circumcising his son brought on a lesson from God that neither he nor Zipporah could ignore. The spilling of the son's blood at his circumcision covered over the sin of his own father. The boy's blood saved Moses' life!

Sound familiar? We, too, face death without a blood sacrifice to provide the transforming power required for our crushing to produce wine. But God has always had a plan for how to address this requirement, once and for all. He would send his first-born and only begotten Son to be our necessary representation before him. In turn, that same Son would be the representation of God before us. Instead of us dying and being doomed to an eternity apart from him, Christ became our sacrificial Lamb, whose blood was spilled and smeared upon the doors of our hearts.

Jesus became our unrighteousness and illegitimacy so that we could become his righteousness and be accepted in the beloved by God. So when death, justice, and the law came calling for us to remunerate the payment of our sin debt, God looked upon all of us who would receive the blood of the Lamb as our substitute and say, "They look like the Lamb. Death has already visited that house!"

The blood of the firstborn, unblemished Son of God saved our lives! The spilling of the eternal, blood-red wine of our Master was poured out like a drink offering on our behalf. Your crushing can become divine wine because the price has been paid by Christ's blood on the cross. Your price has been paid and God's power is at work in your crushing.

The spilling of the eternal, blood-red wine of our Master was poured out like a drink offering on our behalf.

CHAPTER 9

A Vat Full of Wait

The principle part of faith is patience.
—George MacDonald

Some years after I finally accepted my calling, I remember pleading with God to allow me to preach. It was one thing to not even want the calling in the first place. But to be called and then be forced to sit in the background and listen to people speak from books of the Bible they couldn't even properly pronounce was the most aggravating experience of my life. It was during my inner court period that the Lord was developing my gift. I would be in the shower, preaching to bars of soap and washrags.

I would be walking through the woods of West Virginia, laying hands on trees. All of this might sound comical to you, but I now see these moments as part of a season of fermentation.

I spent years cleaning out the baptismal pool and leading devotional services before worship began, wondering when it would be my time to stand and proclaim the infallible Word of God. My heart would ache because I knew I had something to offer. Like the disciples, my heart was rent because the process didn't happen like I wanted.

But waiting was far more beneficial because the Lord was working on something marvelous in a secret place. He was working on my character. He was working on my heart. He was working on my nervousness. He was working on my motives. He was working on my wisdom. He was working on *me*, boiling off every single impurity because there was no way God was going to present to the world an unrefined, unfermented, underdeveloped product.

There was no way God was going to present to the world an unrefined, unfermented, underdeveloped product.

I was a minister for seven years before I preached my first sermon, and I had hundreds of messages lined up and ready to go. But the Lord had me in a holding pattern, and it felt like it would never end. All of it was for a reason, and I didn't realize the greater reason—the wine reason—until Bishop Carlton Pearson called me to speak at Azusa. I preached a sermon there that was later seen by Paul Crouch. Paul Crouch saw only a piece of that sermon on television, but it was during a trying, pressing, and crushing time in his own life. It was just by God's handiwork and timing that Paul saw that one part of my sermon being played and, from there, he called me and invited me to be on TBN.

Shock and Aftershock

I know we're focused on making wine from our crushing, but allow me to borrow a term from another phenomenon that reflects an equally destabilizing change. I have never experienced an earthquake in the full force of its immediacy, but I have visited many locales where the shifting of tectonic plates below the earth's surface resulted in a cataclysmic readjustment, often at the expense of lost lives and pulverized homes and businesses. Scientists use the term *aftershock* to describe the ongoing tremors occurring as a result of the initial quake. Sometimes the aftershock can seem just as damaging, if not more so, as the primary shift.

As we consider the way crushing levels us with what we may feel like a quake deep within our souls, I believe the word *aftershock* aptly describes our emotional state after experiencing the trauma of being crushed. Like the earth experiences smaller quakes after the primary convulsion, we often find ourselves being riddled with the emotional disturbances that come from being reminded of what we've just endured.

Unfortunately, because our mental states have yet to settle, the slightest rattle sends us into a sort of mental overresponsiveness that makes us brace for something else just as terrible as the initial jolt. It's quite similar to post-traumatic stress disorder and leaves us reeling in the wake of our crushing, wondering when the next blow will bruise us. We struggle to hope as we brace for what we expect to be the next infliction of pain upon our psyche.

We're sensitive and scared, anxious about what else might befall us. Just like in our pruning stage, we grapple with how the Vintner who professes to love us so immensely is the same one who initiates such ghastly and dreadful pain. The absence of turmoil seems tenuous, needing only a slight shift to tear the paper-thin semblance of peace that surrounds us after the first quake. We think the quiet is too good to be true, but we're glad all the hell in our lives appears to be over. Yet, our hearts tremble with apprehension and the foreboding feeling that the other shoe will drop in a few seconds. So, repeating what we always do in every moment of transition, we attempt to grab hold of anything in order to stabilize ourselves.

Only this time, something is different. There is little or nothing to hold on to because the damage from the first disturbance was completely catastrophic. What lies around us now are the remains of a life and identity we once knew, because we mistakenly tied everything we were to what we built. Shards of shattered dreams line the landscape as far as we can see, and it's difficult—if not impossible—for us to even think about how we would go about rebuilding what we just lost because of the fear of the later tremblings that must surely be on their way.

This is the fear of a mind and soul trying to find its perch and reassert its trust in the Master that mentioned knowing the end plans and designs He has for our lives. But, if you are honest and anything like me, you must admit to harboring some anger at everything that has happened. You thought you were doing the right thing by producing what you believed to be healthy fruit. Now, what you've labored so long to build has been squashed under the foot of the One who loves you.

Your New Normal Is Never Normal

But notice your emotions amid the process. You feel the way you do because you have lost something that you deem valuable. But to the Vintner, *you* are the one that holds value. Therefore, the way you feel is based on your attachment to what you were doing instead of your inner being, your character that the Master holds so dear. Could it be that your attachment to your achievements would block you from becoming the wine He knows you could be, and that His crushing of those items was for you to recognize that they weren't what really made you who you are?

To the Vintner, you *are the one that holds value.*

Recall that *you* are the fruit, not the product of your labors in all that you have done. Seeing that you are still alive and growing stronger, the Vintner is not done with you yet. The aftershocks, then, are not to be feared because the Master has accomplished in the crushing all that He needed to do to bring you to the stage you currently occupy.

It's here that the Vintner welcomes you to the "what now?" stage of fermentation, that stage in which God is performing more work on you than you can imagine. Often during this apparent rebuilding phase you're confused, because it seems as if nothing is being done at all. You grapple to find a new normal, knowing that you will never be the same and nothing will ever seem normal again. So what should you do with yourself?

At least two people in the Bible can attest to this in-between feeling: David and Jesus. In order for us to better understand fermentation and what it accomplishes, let's consider the process of patient potency experienced by these two in order to understand the process we, too, endure as part of our fermentation into divine wine.

When it comes to winemaking, the fermentation stage is nothing more than a waiting area for the grapes. They have already been crushed, and now the grapes find themselves in an aspect of the process where there is no pain, so to speak. It's a holding pattern, just like when you see a plane waiting for the weather to clear so it can take off or for the runway to be made ready for the plane to land. Some holding patterns can last a matter of minutes, while others could be hours. It's a continuous circling before settling, or stirring around and around in the same vat while nothing seems to be happening.

This is precisely how one feels in the transition phases of life. They're tempted to say there isn't much taking place, but they fail to realize that their movement has progressed. They might find themselves in a holding pattern but fail to understand that their flight has been moved from fortieth in line to second. This is because transition doesn't feel like work; it often feels like waiting. Like climbing a set of steps in a stairwell and finding yourself stuck as one foot hovers above the next step, you're in the position of being able to move up and forward but finding that there's something else to be done before you are fully prepared to complete your climb. It's in that transitory moment of waiting that God is preparing you for the next step.

Just like in a holding pattern, the true work is hidden. A plane's pilot, not fully knowing what's going on on the ground, can only be patient while those in the air traffic control tower work out all the details. Otherwise, the plane might descend before the pilot has been given permission and slam into another jet that is taking off. Destruction comes swiftly on the heels of moving too soon. So, after crushing us, God exercises His grace by allowing us to ferment in the supposed stillness of transition so that we might be ready for the next stage.

The Second Day

Jesus Himself showed us the supreme example of this fermentation process. When we take our provision from the Master by partaking of the bread, which is his Body, we allow the Holy Spirit to shine through us as our prayers are purified by the Spirit making intercession for us. And because all of this is happening beyond the view of others in a private, intimate space, I suspect this is precisely what Jesus was doing on our behalf when He was absent from His body while in the tomb. His mortal body was deceased but in a holding pattern while His soul and spirit were at work elsewhere.

On the first day of His ordeal on our behalf, Christ suffered on the cross, died, and was buried. And on the third day, we know He returned to life and rose again. When the women came to minister to his corpse that morning of the third day, the tomb was empty. But what about the second day? What happened then?

We know from Scripture (Eph. 4:8-10 and Rom.

10:7) that Jesus descended into the place of the dead after His body was crushed for us on the cross. But when He ascended into Heaven as our eternal High Priest, He went to the heavenly reality of which the earthly tabernacle, with its Holy of Holies, was a mere shadow. Of course, every earthly tabernacle is nothing more than a shadow because as we have seen in God's instructions to Moses (in Exodus 25:40) was that he make everything according to pattern.

Remember that what happened in the inner court of the tabernacle was not seen by all. Similarly, the transformation process from death back to life occurred in the darkness of the tomb. When I consider this, I cannot help but imagine how helpless the disciples must have felt. To them, their king was dead. It is likely they believed that the presence of the Messiah would usher in a new way of life for all Jews, thinking that Jesus would overthrow their Roman oppressors and set up a new, earthly kingdom through which He would govern the entire world. All of their ideas, thoughts, and hopes for the future shattered when Jesus died.

The transformation process from death back to life occurred in the darkness of the tomb.

The disciples' descent into despair got even more desperate. To even be considered someone who followed Jesus was an automatic death warrant. So scared were Jesus' followers for their lives that they initially went into hiding, huddling in rooms and out-of-the-way places for fear that they would face Caiaphas next and be crucified. With all your hopes lost, knowing full well that you were next in line for the most excruciating death possible, it might begin to make sense that you would deny knowing Christ as well. Because, when the chips are down and your back is pressed against the wall without any light shining on you or your situation, you're seemingly willing to do anything to survive.

But for those who know the Lord, our survival is not limited to our own ability. In fact, as we have seen, our survival relies on our willingness to surrender. We begin to recognize this in-between moment of time is transitory and transitional. We're experiencing spiritual growing pains.

Jesus' time in the tomb wasn't permanent. A change was happening in the silence and darkness of the tomb, and just because you can't see it with your naked eye does not mean the Master isn't working on your behalf. Just because you can't perceive what is taking place in the inner court of your divine destiny doesn't mean that work isn't being done there. Just because you lost everything during your crushing in the outer court does not mean that nothingness is what you must anticipate for the rest of your life. The very fact that you've gained entrance into the inner court suggests that crushing could never be the end of what God has in store for you.

So before you lose your mind and give up, before you throw in the towel and walk away from your dream, before you let your faith slip away, I suggest you do something that all of us hate to do. It's something the disciples were forced to do when everything they looked forward to seemed to turn to ashes. They had to do it even when Peter spoke of returning to fishing. They had to do it when they were huddled together for their lives. They were pushed to do it as the stone was rolled in front of the opening of Jesus' tomb.

They were forced to wait.

Stirred while Shaken

Perhaps it's human nature, but I fear it only gets worse with each passing generation: we hate to wait. We've all been trained to get everything *now*. We have to buy now, move now, eat now, lead now, talk now, text now, enjoy now. We need the marriage now. We need the family now. We must have our company and business now. We want the fulfillment of our destinies *right now*, never minding the fact that God's grace is extended to us by allowing us to ferment in the holding pattern.

Although it may feel like it will never end, our fermentation is really just a brief time of transition. Life won't always be like this. Even in the face of the small amount of work that you can accomplish in the inner court after being crushed outside, the only thing the Vintner is requiring you to do is exercise patience. The ingredients are in place. You have been crushed and your juice extracted. Now it's time to let the divine process of transformation unfold.

When I first began penning this book, I was intrigued that God compelled me to build my message around the process of winemaking. Yes, I know that wine figures heavily throughout Scripture and points us to the work of the Holy Spirit. But at first this metaphor of maximization seemed too simple to me. But then I realized that's exactly why God wants me to use it. Yes, wine is simple but God's Word tells us that He chose the foolish things of the world to shame the wise (Cor. 1:27).

CRUSHING

Wine figures heavily throughout Scripture and points us to the work of the Holy Spirit.

Winemaking basically comes down to three steps: crushing the grapes, allowing the juice to ferment, and collecting the wine. In other words, you mash the fruit, allow the juice to sit, and enjoy the results. That's it. Of course, there are other things that vintners have learned to do throughout history to refine and enhance their wines, but it takes little to no technology to create this beverage that humanity has enjoyed for thousands of years. The procedure is simple, direct, and to the point.

Particularly when it comes to fermentation, the process is rather straightforward. Fermentation is nothing more than the process in which the sugar in fruit is converted to alcohol because of its interaction with the natural yeast within its skins. After the grapes were crushed, a vintner in Jewish antiquity would allow the grapes and their juices to remain in their vats and ferment in the open air. As the yeast acted upon the sugar, it would produce a faint hissing sound similar to boiling. This resulted from the reaction in which carbon dioxide was released in the process. Apparently, some people who remained too close to the vats would be rendered unconscious. There are even reports of people being knocked out by the gases, then falling and drowning in fermenting wine.

Though fermentation is simple, the process is not to be disrespected. It still requires the vintner to keep a careful watch on the vats so that the wine does not turn to vinegar. You see, if too much time passes, the juice becomes bitter. Though some would allow the grapes to remain in the vats, other vintners would opt to place the fermenting juice in jars. Either way, the forthcoming wine was watched closely.

Carbon dioxide is a waste product expelled from organisms after a chemical reaction occurs. For instance, each time you exhale, you are releasing carbon dioxide. This expulsion shows us something valuable. The longer you hold on to that which you should release, the more dangerous it is to you. Suffocation could be the result, putting an abrupt end to something that should have continued to exist in another form. I suggest, then, that the fermentation process God takes us through acts as a spiritual broom He uses to sweep away what we no longer need. After all, in the midst of transformation, there must be a casting off of the old and adherence to all that is new. One must give way to the other, for they cannot coexist.

Taste over Haste

But what about the toxicity of what we release? The negativity we carry in our hearts can be so ugly, adverse, and contrary to what God has called us to be. If these dregs are not dealt with in short order, they easily become communicable and spread throughout the nearby population like an unstoppable poison. Perhaps, then, this is why the Master Vintner allows our fermentation to take place outside the view, influence, and input of others. For if people get too close to us during the process of casting off everything we have failed to release over the years, those same people can easily be rendered spiritually unconscious, never wanting to have anything to do with us *or* the Vintner we wish to emulate.

I cannot properly express to you my gratitude for the Lord having the wisdom to relocate me to private places, hiding me within His wings as He went to work on my character. I've learned the hard way that many people cannot handle the ugly parts of me. If you're honest with yourself, I gather that you would arrive at the same conclusion about yourself. As a matter of fact, I'll bet that you've caught glimpses of how black-hearted you can be and were completely caught off guard and left thinking, *I had no clue I could be that rude.*

This is because transition isn't easy.

During times of change, upheaval, and transition, you become moody, unstable, emotionally irregular, and sometimes even contemptible. I know I can become all of those and more. This is why you have to be careful with people while they're changing. You have to be mature and ready for whatever comes, because when the truth is told, you never know what you're going to get. So be cautious with how you handle someone who's in the midst of change—including yourself. As God works within us, we all throw off noxious material. We are being refined for a greater purpose than anyone can imagine or understand.

We are being refined for a greater purpose than anyone can imagine or understand.

Instead of despairing or fearing God's absence, we must appreciate the grace the Vintner is showing us when He hides us in the Inner Court during our fermenting times, those times when all things dead are in the tomb while transition occurs. We all experience seasons that are like the second day. Waiting. Wondering. Waiting some more.

It's not just so that someone else won't get hurt while you're being transformed; it's also that *you* won't be corrupted. How pitiful it would be for the Master Vintner to return to the vats and see the vintage He *knew* would be the best He has ever produced actually be worse than vinegar because something soured during the fermentation period. Or what if he released you too soon?

Whatever it is the Master has placed on your heart to do for Him, I would suggest that He has, or will, take you through a season of hiding you. It's there that He gets you ready for your assignment. And you wouldn't be the first. Joseph was hidden in the pit and in prisons. Moses was hidden in the desert for forty years. David was hidden in the pastures while tending sheep. Jesus was hidden in Egypt as a child long before He endured His time in the tomb. Each of them was locked away and tended only by the Master Vintner, lest someone came along and disrupt their maturation process on the way to becoming wine.

I thank God for hiding me and releasing me when He was ready instead of when I was still fermenting. No matter how ready I thought I was to preach and move into the next level of my ministry, the Lord knew the time I needed to ferment and mature. His timing rarely seems to match our own impatience, but we must learn to release our haste in order to experience taste.

Too many of us rush to get to the end of the process, trying to tell God that we are ready for what He has for us when we've not even fully understood the giftings He has placed in us. Or we would be waiting and rehearsing when our time comes for the spotlight to shine on us as life's curtain goes up.

His timing may not reflect our expectations, but during fermentation we must practice patience and trust His perfect knowledge of the time required for us to reach maximum potency and flavor. The Master Vintner knows when your wine is ready. He knows when your fermentation is done.

During fermentation we must practice patience and trust His perfect knowledge of the time required for us to reach maximum potency and flavor.

You don't have to rush the process.
You don't have to rush Him.
You *can't* rush Him!
How can a grape and its juice ever know when they have become wine? The grapes don't know

they've been changed into something eternal because they're still grappling with the temporal and physical pain they've just endured. But in the midst of all their struggle, they've become something the Master is now ready to taste.

After letting the transitional process of fermentation have its way, the Master Vintner takes a draw from the vat, knowing that His work has paid off. With the goblet and His hand stained red with the new wine, He brings it to His nose to smell it and savor the scent that wafts upward. And for what feels like an eternity, He enjoys the aromatic bouquet produced after our crushing.

CHAPTER 10

Out of the Tomb and into the Bottle

One can choose to go back toward safety or forward toward growth. Growth must be chosen again and again; fear must be overcome again and again.
—*Abraham Maslow*

In the past year, my wife began complaining about having severe abdominal pain, and while several doctors had treated her, none could find its source. Meanwhile, the pain persisted and increased in intensity and severity. Even though she continued to attend church services and move around the house, Serita was clearly in excruciating discomfort. Finally, we found a doctor who provided the correct diagnosis involving the cause within her body. After trying simple solutions to resolve the problem, it became apparent surgery was necessary.

And I dreaded it.

I dreaded it not because I feared it was life-threatening. My concern emerged from the fact that Serita is unable to take normal post-operation medications due to allergies to most painkillers. So we had several discussions with her doctor about how to manage her pain, both prior to surgery as well as in recovery. The good news was that the surgery itself would only require her to be hospitalized for a day before she could return home. The recovery process, however, required about six weeks. After that, she would be good as new and healthier than ever.

The timing of this situation, though, was far from ideal.

As soon as the doctor prescribed surgery to eradicate the problem, my wife and I realized that her recovery period would coincide directly with our youngest son's college graduation. We tried to configure our calendar to include both events, but it was impossible. So after much discussion and deliberation, Serita said, "I will endure whatever pain I feel until I can have the surgery. But I am not about to miss seeing Dexter graduate from college! Oh, no, Satan will not steal this moment from me!"

She was going to be there if there was breath in her body. While I knew better than to argue with her, over the following month I watched her endure some of the most unbearable pain I've ever witnessed. We tried everything possible to modulate and remediate her body's distress, with little or no impact.

Eventually, my wife no longer went to church and seldom left the bedroom. I cancelled all my engagements to be with her. I cooked her favorite meals, which she barely touched, and tried to clean the house and care for her as best I could. When we made it to Dexter's graduation, she could barely walk, but she held on to me, climbed on that plane, and we flew to California to watch our son walk across the stage at his college's commencement ceremony. Somehow we made it to the event venue and found our seats. I continued to be impressed at the strength of someone I already admired for her tenacity, stamina, and willpower.

We flew home immediately after the graduation ceremony and went directly to the hospital the next morning. The surgery took five hours. Her doctor came to me afterward and told me the procedure had been very successful. He felt confident of her recovery and the resolution of her pain.

The next day she was back home, and for a brief period, all the pain she had been suffering stopped completely—only to be replaced by the pain of recovery. You see, all pain is not the same. The pain that led to surgery seemed to have no purpose, only to warn of imminent danger and ultimate death. The pain after surgery, however, provided a different message, communicating the restoration of her body as she healed.

Recovery can be painful.

Fermentation takes time.

And then moving new wine from the vat into the bottle also requires time.

So does moving from the cross to the empty tomb.

Moving new wine from the vat into the bottle also requires time.

Carry Your Cross

The cross was a familiar symbol that was common to the Roman's method of execution. Even after His crucifixion, it was quite some time before the cross became associated with worship and beloved by Christians. In Jesus' time, it had the equivalent connotation to what we might associate with the gas chamber, waterboarding, or death row. Mentioning death by crucifixion conjured a sense of shame and degradation, embarrassment and horror. Only the most heinous criminals, those who had either brutally offended society or those who had no one to come to their defense, were nailed to two rough-hewn beams of wood and left there to suffer in agony until they died.

Even after Jesus returned from the dead and left His empty tomb, the cross continued to be an emblem heard only in hushed whispers in the early church. One of my favorite hymns, "The Old Rugged Cross," would not have been a song early followers of Jesus sang to celebrate the Savior's death and resurrection. Instead of a wondrous symbol of eternal victory over sin and death, those first Christians still consider the cross a reminder of their temporary loss and the devastating anguish they felt during those three long days before Christ rose from the dead.

While I appreciate that we now use the cross as a symbol of worship and recognize its significance of Jesus' sacrifice on our behalf, I fear we may denigrate the suffering of the cross by not recognizing its crushing weight at the time. The cross's crushing power was both literal as well as figurative. Two of the gospel accounts (Mark 15:21 and Luke 23:26) mention how a man was apparently plucked from the crowd and forced by the Roman guards to help carry the cross on Jesus' bloodied shoulders: "As the soldiers led Him away, they seized Simon from Cyrene, who was on his way in from the country, and put the cross on Him and made Him carry it behind Jesus" (Luke 23:26).

I recall visiting Jerusalem and walking along the ancient cobblestone road that connects the Antonia Fortress near the Temple Mount—where Paul would later deliver a sermon (Acts 21:37) with Golgotha, the hill of the skull, where Christ was nailed to His cross, a location so instilled in history that all four gospels mention it (Matthew 27:33, Mark 15:22, Luke 23:33, and John 19:17). This route is traditionally believed to be the path Jesus followed and is called Via Dolorosa, which is Latin for "Way of Suffering."

Walking that hilly, crooked, narrow road, I could not help but wonder at the torture of carrying such tangible weight as the cross, which must have weighed hundreds of pounds. A healthy person would struggle to uphold such a burden and transport it across the jagged stony path, let alone one who had been beaten, berated, and broken like our Lord. Experiencing that walk made the reality of the cross just a little more palpable.

Because of the familiarity of the cross to us as believers, though, I worry it has been reduced in its impact, as common as any other emblem, symbol, or brand icon. When the story of Jesus' death and resurrection becomes as familiar as Aesop's fables, we overlook how it must have been for the disciples who pulled His rigor mortis–ridden body down from the tree and forced His stiff arms to rest across His chest as they felt the coldness of His skin and hardness of His body. The hands that once healed the sick and the feet that walked on water felt as cold and lifeless as the stones along the Via Dolorosa.

He was gone. And with His death so were their dreams. Their Master was gone, and there were no more discussions about who would sit on the right side or the left. He was gone. And they must have wondered what would become of them, these men who had spent three years away from their families, their jobs, their careers, for a kingdom that ended up on a cross?

Like the crushing of the grapes, that which was so beautiful, the Messiah, the Word Made Flesh, the Incarnation, was reduced to a lifeless corpse. Just before they're crushed, right when they're at their peak, blushed with ripe, juicy, sun-drenched flavor, filled with sweetness and nectar unlike any other, grapes become shells, remnants of their former uncrushed glory. Suddenly, there is no beauty about them at all.

And in those darkest moments as we consider how—not if—we will ever be able to get back up and go on. We know ourselves only as empty husks of the ethereal dreams that once fueled our soul. But as we ferment and become wine, we must never forget that what we once were is nothing compared with what we are becoming.

We must never forget that what we once were is nothing compared with what we are becoming.

Gift from the Grit

I have never known anyone who is incredibly successful who did not have some dark, shameful, horrific place through which they had endured and suffered and agonized, filled with frightful anxiety that they might not survive. And then eventually, slowly and gradually, through tenacity and divine intervention and support from others, they too showed themselves to be alive.

They begin to feel their strength again. They realize they will never be the same—but what if they could go on? What if some diamond could emerge from the crushing weight applied to their soul? What if some priceless pearl could be extracted from the shell of who they once were?

When Jesus arose from the dead, it was the women who first saw the burial shroud crumpled like a sleeper's discarded blankets from the One who had awakened from death back into life. These women were the first, not because they were so filled with faith that they expected to find such a sight. No, they had come to their beloved Master's tomb out of loyalty, to decorate the stench with incense and myrrh.

But their loyalty and devotion intrigue me. They expressed no disappointment about placement, position, or politics. They refused to complain about their vulnerable investment in this spiritual venture that now seemed to mock them from the cross. No, these women remained loyal to what He used to be, not expecting anything else but to protect His image from passersby, to afford one last act of love and respect to Jesus of Nazareth.

Imagine their surprise and dismay and confusion when they found that there was no corpse, no body, no sign of Him. The grave had been disrupted. The stone had been rolled away. He was not there. What did this mean?

They carried the message back to the men. The first carriers of the gospel news were women. And it was not met with rejoicing, because who would believe something so fantastical? You can go so low that people won't believe you can come out, so their news was met with disbelief and barely a skeptic's curiosity. Peter and John ran down to see if it could be true or just another silly fabrication.

They entered, and...nothing! They backed up out of the grave, astonished at what they saw. He had risen. Not what they expected and yet...surely, their minds must have gone into overdrive as they attempted to process this shocking, unthinkable turn of events. All the moments with their Master suddenly had to be revisited, reviewed, and recalibrated. Was this what Jesus meant all along?

Christ not only rose from the dead for each individual's salvation, but He also returned to bring resurrection power through the Holy Spirit to us collectively, as His body, His bride, the fellowship of believers known as the church. Most theologians and church historians consider Pentecost the turning point for the birth of the church. At Pentecost, believers gathered together for prayer and worship and received the gift of the Holy Spirit infusing their minds, their hearts, and their bodies with divine resurrection power.

And when we start talking about the glorious power of the Pentecost that birthed the church, we must realize that Pentecost sets its watch from the bloody desolate place of the Passover. Pentecost was a place where the harvesters gathered to bring in the sheaves and reap the benefits of the toil of their labor. Only fifty days from the bloody tipping point of time and history, Pentecost revealed the gift emerging from God's most precious sacrifice.

See for Yourself

This birth of Christianity at Pentecost and the growth and evolution of the early church continue to fascinate me. I don't know any other faith that uses such a horrific image as an emblem of hope, such a despicable symbol as a beloved indicator of their devotion. I cannot help but wonder if perhaps the cross reminds us that without crushing there is no wine, without crucifixion there is no crown, without pain no power, without suffering no success.

He showed Himself alive for forty days with many infallible proofs, not to convince a world that had already made up its mind, not to persuade the Romans who thought they had resolved the problem, but to indelibly brand His flock with this powerful, profound point that crushing is not the end.

Jesus showed Himself to be alive because it's important for people to see that there is something on the other side of poverty, shame, disgrace, suffering, and death. You see, it would not have been enough for Him to be resurrected if there were no witnesses. They had to see the tomb was empty.

Jesus showed Himself to be alive because it's important for people to see that there is something on the other side of poverty, shame, disgrace, suffering, and death.

Witnesses of His living, breathing, resurrected body birthed the church, and the impact of His crushing spread from them across the world. Christ revealed Himself among them for just under five weeks to show Himself to be alive at various places, points, and times to burn into their thinking that this process that they witnessed has purpose—purpose bigger than reversing their own disappointment and disbelief. Perhaps it was because He knew they too would have crosses to bear, pains to be endured, and shame from which to be unshackled. Maybe it was because of His omniscient awareness of what you and I and those around us are going through at this very moment.

After all, you and I share in our own personal pains and crises and dilemmas and say we are believers, but what is it to believe if we do not believe that there is something beyond the pain that we may feel at this moment? What is the point? We must see the living, risen Christ for ourselves.

When we face the darkest moments of our lives, there is something on the other side of it.

Paul says it is hope that makes us not ashamed (Rom. 5:5). Hope promises that there's something on the other side of shame that is an antidote to it. If we have no hope, then we are of all people most miserable.

There's shame in every bad decision, divorce, bankruptcy, scandal, resignation, unplanned birth, and exposed immorality. But if we can drink from the cup of hope, then this present suffering is not worthy to be compared with the glory that shall be revealed in us. So when we remember Jesus' body and blood at the Lord's supper, we lift up the cup filled with wine and not only commemorate His death but also celebrate His resurrection. Only by crushing can those grapes become wine in that very cup.

Vineyard to Victory

We have seen how the grapes must be crushed to produce wine, but how exactly did the cross become the much-beloved symbol of our faith? Doing a bit of research, I discovered that Helen, the mother of the emperor Constantine during the fourth century, allegedly went on a quest to find the actual cross upon which Jesus had died. She searched the known world until she found what she believed to be the antique wooden artifact, which had started to splinter and crack. But what to do with it? How could she spread the gospel once she found what she had been looking for?

Helen took various slivers and splinters of the wood and sent them to believers and churches around the world. With these wooden fragments, people around the world began venerating the cross and contemplating its reality. Seeing part of the actual cross caused people to pray and worship. Gradually, the cross began to represent something sacred, sacrificial, and sacramental.

Prior to Helen's quest and distribution, the cross only marked a place of agony. But as its presence spread thanks to Helen, the cross became an emblem of Christ's crushing and the new wine produced when He emerged from the tomb. The cross went from an artifact of atrocity to become an icon of adoration.

The cross became an emblem of Christ's crushing and the new wine produced when He emerged from the tomb.

Such a transformation is itself a crucial message. Imagine if the electric chair or gas chamber had people kneeling around it with no thought of the horrific purpose it once held! But in effect, this is exactly what happened with the cross. No other religion in history has ever used an emblem of horror for its enduring brand.

Think of any other religion, country, or company that would advertise its shame and horror and use it as a brand, and yet we have many Christians who seem shocked when we go through hard times. The whole brand, though, is about overcoming shame.

Our weeping endures for a night, but joy comes in the morning. Whether we want to or not, all of us must pick up some kind of cross and follow Jesus into suffering.

And how people's perception of the cross changed stands out just as dramatically. Helen's actions as much as anyone's caused the good news to be spread and accepted all over the world. Isn't it ironic that God used a woman to transform how we see the cross, just as He used women to carry the message of Christ's resurrection back to the men, and yet we still debate where and when and how God can use women to minister. How striking that if not for women, the story would not have broken in the first place. Women at that time lived in such a misogynistic society that I can't help but think they related to

Jesus because of His own crushing. There is a fellowship among those who know the pain of suffering.

Yes, we all have our crosses to bear. A failed marriage, a special needs child, a debilitating injury, a chronic illness, unbearable debt. We all go through crushing, but we must never forget crushing is not the end. We go from the vineyard to the vat to the victory.

But clinging to that truth can be so hard when everything around you is slipping away. When I married my wife, I had a car, a good job, and a place to stay. But shortly after I said "I do," my car was totaled, my company had shut down, and I found myself struggling to buy food to feed our family. We used paper towels and duct tape to make diapers for our kids. We returned soda bottles and cans for enough change to wrap until we had a full roll so we could buy a few groceries. I can remember stopping along the side of the road to pick up apples beneath a tree at the edge of the woods. I will never forget the nights I stared up at the sky and wondered if we would ever get beyond our struggles.

I'll never forget coming home from church one night and finding that Appalachian Power had turned off the power in our house. I couldn't bear to tell our kids, so young at the time, why we were in the dark, so instead I improvised on the spot and told them it was a game. I had turned off all the lights and whoever could get into bed without stubbing their toes would win. I didn't want my children to grow up poor and feel limited by that awareness. I wanted them to know it was possible to be people of color and have more than what I was able to show them at that time. I didn't know how, but I knew I had to endure beyond the crushing and trust there was life beyond this tomb.

A few years later, when I wrote my first book and my ministry was taking off, I bought a beautiful home with an indoor swimming pool, which was ironic because I couldn't swim. But I would pull up a chair and watch my kids splash and play, and it gave me the greatest joy to show them there was more. I wished my father could have lived long enough to witness such a sight and enjoy the wine now being opened from the crushing he had endured for my sake.

He used to take our family for rides on Sunday afternoons, cruising through posh white neighborhoods to point out the houses that he cleaned during the week. He would describe the particular rugs and drapes of each one, the furniture and color of the rooms. Many of them often had the little black jockey statues near the driveway or in the manicured gardens. I remember wondering what we would put in our yards or set at the edge of our driveways someday if we ever had a home so palatial.

I'm not the only one who struggles to see life beyond the tomb. I remember visiting Coretta Scott King once and admiring her plush apartment in Atlanta. When her house blew up decades before and the force of it knocked her back against the kitchen wall, she could not have known that one day she would be sharing the trauma as a story of survival from a luxurious home high above the city where her life was once endangered. But as her crushing fermented into the wine of experience, wisdom, and influence, she discovered a flavor she could not have anticipated at the time of her crushing.

As her crushing fermented into the wine of experience, wisdom, and influence, she discovered a flavor she could not have anticipated at the time of her crushing.

Even after your pain has fermented and you find yourself in a new location, a new job, a new relationship, or a new lifestyle, you will still struggle. Like wine being poured from the vat into the bottles in order to be shipped and purchased and consumed, we must learn to be contained by new shapes. Jesus said, "No one sews a patch of unshrunk cloth on an old garment, for the patch will pull away from the garment, making the tear worse. Neither do people pour new wine into old wineskins. If they do, the skins will burst; the wine will run out and the wineskins will be ruined. No, they pour new wine into new wineskins, and both are preserved." (Matt. 9:16–17).

New Wineskins

Rather than contain our new wine in bottles, I fear some people never make it out of the vats of fermentation. Too often, in our country and its present culture, crushing has become a hopeless cycle from which there is no escape. If you're crushed long enough, you accept that weight as your reality rather than a temporary predicament. You make yourself comfortable in a crushing place and you never really believe that crushing is not the end.

Whether one is a starving Middle Eastern child, a single mother raising her children on the south side of Chicago, or someone living in the rough parts of Soweto in South Africa, it's never easy. If you've never seen anyone who looks like you who's made it, then the crushing stays and becomes your world. Everyone from your bubble who escapes and comes back to leave clues, however, drives home to the next generation that it is at least possible to break through the crushing.

When I listen to current debates about Rust Belt states and the forlorn abandonment they feel after industry shutdown and local companies closed and their residents' frantic need to get someone in the White House who heard them, I understand their desperation.

I go into the inner cities of Chicago, Baltimore, and Los Angeles, and even though these urban dwellers may not know or even like their counterparts in the heartlands, both share and express the same despair, the trauma of being nailed to a cross from which they cannot be freed, forgotten like the crushed pulp of a grape left behind to rot.

Being from West Virginia and married to a coal miner's daughter, I watched the nice brick homes of miners and their families disintegrate to ramshackle abodes and raggedy trailers. Poverty, like bigotry itself, respects no one and can consume anyone. If we assume that the plight of others can never touch us, then we're as naïve as the cities that once believed the Ebola virus could never contaminate their communities. Until we realize our shared condition, we will never really be free.

The process of transformation for all of us begins with each of us. After we have endured our crushing, after some time has passed and we have experienced a perspective fermenting our pain into personal power, we must then begin our life as new wine. We must accept that nothing will ever be the same again. We cannot reclaim, repair, or recycle that which has been lost or broken. We must begin again knowing that we have new wine to offer. Like Lazarus returned to life and leaving the tomb, we must unwrap the burial cloths from our bodies.

The process of transformation for all of us begins with each of us.

It's time to stop living in the past.

It's time to leave your tomb behind.

It's time to taste the new wine God is producing in your life.

CHAPTER II

Spiritual Fermentation

Spending time with God puts everything else in perspective.

—R. A. Torrey

The Temple Mount was abuzz with energy from all the tourists who descended upon the most visited site in Israel. Three Abrahamic faiths—Judaism, Christianity, and Islam—though divergent in how they approach God, intersect with one another at this location. There is a unifying effect about the Temple Mount, causing most of the people who visit the site to treat one another with dignity and respect. Of course, should anyone have become irate, I'm sure the well-armed security guards would have been more than happy to remind any and all upstarts of their place and remove them if necessary.

Without a single cloud in the azure sky, the day sparkled like a sunlit jewel. It was my first time visiting Jerusalem, and I couldn't have prayed for better weather. My family and I were nearing the Western Wall, the only remaining structure of what used to be Herod's temple. Better known to others as the Wailing Wall, it stands just over sixty feet high and was sixteen hundred feet long. The entire court was littered with tourists who took photos and those who merely sought to obtain a personal glimpse of the holiest site in Judaism.

Along with several other points of interest about the Wall, two stood out to me. One dealt with a curious tradition of people writing their prayers on paper and inserting them into the cracks of the wall. Having journeyed from my home halfway around the world, I knew there wasn't a chance that I would miss the opportunity to write my own prayer and contribute to the more than a million prayers brought to the Wall every year. While I understand that I'm able to pray anywhere and anytime and know the Master hears even my indiscernible moans and grunts, I would be lying to you if I told you that I didn't feel a powerful flood of emotions as I placed my own hand-scrawled prayer within one of the Wall's crevices.

Other than the Sepulcher, Golgotha, and Via Dolorosa, the Wailing Wall was one of those places during my tour of Jerusalem that brought tears to my eyes. To know that I walked where Jesus stood, taught, died, and was buried brought out feelings within me that even my own extensive vocabulary cannot describe. It was enough to make me break out in spontaneous worship of the Master, and I'm quite sure that I wasn't the only one who felt that way.

I placed my prayer in the Wall, but as I backed away, I noticed the second thing about the site that held my attention captive: the Orthodox Jews visiting the Wall. Like everyone else, they brought their prayers, chose a fissure, and inserted them. Among their other rituals of praying there, they captured my attention in how they moved their bodies. As they prayed, each of them rocked back and forth, continuously moving. Thinking back on my own personal conversations with God, I could not remember a single instance in which I had swayed like they were doing. As a pastor of a mega-ministry, I'm accustomed to those moments when the Holy Spirit takes over. Any movement committed during those times, however, tends to be spontaneous and isn't repeated on a regular basis as, from what I could tell, their actions were.

I turned back to my guide, who stood several feet away, and he noticed my peculiar expression and smiled. Anticipating my question, he said, "They rock as an homage to how God moved with them in the wilderness. Wherever the people of Israel went, Yahweh went with them."

Instantly, my mind and heart sizzled with excitement as the preacher and teacher in me recognized the new sermon the guide had given me in less than five seconds. I chuckled at his response and looked at my wife, who automatically knew what I was thinking: God, the Almighty Creator of the universe, traveled *with* Israel. He lived and moved among His children in the midst of the wilderness, guiding them in their wandering.

God, the Almighty Creator of the universe, traveled with Israel. He lived and moved among His children in the midst of the wilderness, guiding them in their wandering.

Now perhaps this seems inconsequential or esoteric to you, but my mind was spinning with everything that had taken place before the Master even allowed Himself to come close to His chosen people. What intrigues me most about the Lord's characteristics is His willingness to not only move *with* his people, but His penchant for relocating His chosen ones—be it you, me, or another—before He puts His plan into effect.

Can you see why this matters?

God's hand and presence are standing front and center in any and every stage of our crushing.

To look in your days of calamity and not see the One that has promised to never leave you or forsake you is to cause you to abandon hope that life will get any better. So if we see the Orthodox Jews in constant motion while in the midst of their prayers to pay respect to the fact that God was moving with Israel in the wilderness and before the children of Israel were freed from Egypt's grasp, don't their actions beg us to pay attention? Shouldn't we look for God's presence in our own movements and transitions in life? And if we look for Him, how can we find Him?

Perpetual Motion

To answer these questions, I believe we must consider what it means to spend time with God, to get to know Him and to communicate with Him. Though time given to our numerous responsibilities requires our full attention, I quickly learned as an adult that I also need to set aside time for myself and my family.

To give all of yourself to everyone and everything else and leave little, if any, of you to your family and yourself is to do your future and your destiny a grave disservice. There is something to be said about the value of being alone and taking a break from it all. It makes no sense to arrive at the fruition of your destiny and have little to no strength to walk in it.

It's a wonder to me that some individuals hate the concept of being by themselves. They desperately need the presence of others, even if those people are toxic to be around. Of course, humanity is a communal species, and I'm not taking away from that truth. Everyone, however, must learn the value, healing qualities, and even necessity of being alone to rest, recharge, receive divine insight, and purge what has been affecting them. Always being surrounded by people and standing in the presence of others prevents one from experiencing the blessings found only in solitude.

From one whose schedule is often packed with attending back-to-back meetings, keeping myriad appointments, fulfilling speaking engagements, overseeing film and music productions, writing books, counseling others, traveling over and through various time zones, running a mega-ministry, and preaching the Gospel almost every Sunday of the year at the Potter's House, I am here to tell you that you cannot afford not to have downtime. If you think that my wife, Serita, would tolerate me giving every aspect of myself to others and leaving nothing for her and our children, you are grossly mistaken. As a matter of fact, she and my family come first. It's one of the main reasons that she and I have enjoyed over thirty-five years of marriage. Therefore, it is absolutely necessary that I allow myself the luxury of retreating from every demand that my calling and vocation require of me.

You must do the same and make time for rest a priority. Even more to the point, you must discover that certain blessings and assets are found only in rest. Better still, some advantages emerge exclusively in and while being alone. I think my best thoughts when I'm alone, and I move faster without weight of other responsibilities and distractions. Plus, the Father loves to speak, especially when there are no distractions between the two of us.

The Husbandman recognizes the value of seclusion because He values the harvest and wine His fruit will produce. I have noticed that He has the propensity to remove and relocate individuals chosen to complete tasks for His Kingdom from among crowds or familiar environments. It is rare that you see God calling someone to a unique destiny and Him allowing them to remain where they've always been. I'm hard-pressed to think of a single instance.

The Husbandman recognizes the value of seclusion because He values the harvest and wine His fruit will produce.

It's almost as if He wishes to cultivate something within them.

We see this pattern throughout Scripture. Noah, the first vintner, experienced his own loneliness when he was called away to build the Ark. Abraham was told to leave the land of his fathers for a place that God would show him before He brought Abraham into covenant with him. Joseph was sold into slavery by his own brothers and, while away from his family, God trained him to run Egypt. Moses, after having become a murderer, was driven to the wilderness where he meets God and receives His orders to be the voice and deliverer to free the children of Israel. David, considered to be the runt of his family, was alone during his on-the-job training that prepared him to be the king of Israel who would succeed Saul. And we already discussed a microscopic, yet significant, aspect of Jesus' lonely time of pressing in the Garden of Gethsemane. The gospels are replete with instances of Jesus withdrawing to be alone and pray.

To the untrained eye, all of this would seem like

wandering and meandering without a purpose. Could there be more to it, though?

We see that being alone for a season is valuable in God's sight, but I don't want you to harp on the aloneness we have previously discussed. I'm calling your attention to God's penchant to move you into the position and place that is most strategic for His will while you experience a feeling of being lost. He doesn't do this just to prepare you. He does this because the first thing we see God doing when we initially meet Him in the first chapter of Genesis is hovering, brooding, breathing, and moving over the darkness and void that existed before He called the wandering, formless, nothingness to order and commanded light to explode onto the scene.

So what does this tell us?

Quite simply, we do not serve a stagnant, motionless, dormant, inactive, or idle God. From the first time we meet Him, we see that God is always on the move. God's movement suggests progress and purpose. And though He may be silent during certain seasons, we must accept the fact that our God is a perpetually moving God. Now, if we see that God is always moving with purpose, who are we to think that we would be different from the Master who created us? God will move us to accomplish His ultimate goal and purpose in and for our lives.

*God will move us to accomplish His ultimate goal
and purpose in and for our lives.*

As we see God moving, similarly, we see Him moving Jacob (whose name was changed to Israel) and his children into Egypt. There, they mature into a nation. Afterward, God moves them out so that He could develop a relationship with them. He does the same in our own lives. Regardless of the adversities that visit us in our lives, God is still moving on our behalf. I grant you that it might be difficult to trace Him in our times of trouble, but that is when it is absolutely necessary that we trust Him.

Though I don't want you to dwell on being in the alone place with God, we must reach back and grab that concept because we're about to see that God does most of his moving in our lives when we are alone with Him and without distraction. In essence, there is a marriage that exists between the two that is absolutely necessary for us to graduate to the next level in the process of our crushing. For it is in that space of wandering without interference that we begin to discover hints at the Husbandman's will for our lives.

A King on the Move

We must remember that the making of wine is a process. Because of that thought, without hesitation or doubt, I can honestly tell you that God's relocation of you to a place of solitude is so that He can prepare you to do what He has called you to do. If you're looking around at the various aspects of your life and see ubiquitous isolation or seclusion, know that you are being groomed for something special, and the Master wants to interfere in the process. Unfortunately, detachment often carries with it a certain degree of pain because each of us, on some level, requires interaction with another human being. After all, even the Master says it's not good for man to be permanently alone. Thankfully, in those moments when we are to ourselves, God's habit of communicating with us shows itself.

I've already shared some of my personal instances of being up at night, trying to wrap my head around challenging circumstances. But in addition to thinking, feeling, and grieving over the situations that resulted in my restless, sleepless night, I also experienced something else. After getting tired of pacing, I would quiet myself and listen out for God's still, small Voice of direction or correction.

God never failed to speak to me. Oh, He might have waited to do so, but He has never stopped communicating with me. Rather, I discovered that I had to allow God to be God and communicate with me in the manner He thought best for the moment. After silencing the loud angst of my mind, I would hear Him speak words of peace to my troubled soul and provide steps that, once executed, would cause me to wonder why I had worried so much in the first place. I'm telling you that there is something about God's presence and His ability to impart wisdom, identity, and peace in those times of uncertainty.

I discovered that I had to allow God to be God and communicate with me in the manner He thought best for the moment.

Could it be that He was doing the same with Israel when they left Egypt and wandered in the wilderness? Was God using their wandering as a tool to hammer home the point that all we need is him? And, if our necessities are vanquished and we're given purpose and identity in God's presence, is our wandering really wandering? Could our constant moving and wandering actually have a point?

For answers, let's consider yet another, bigger question: What was the purpose of freeing the children of Israel? Slaves have existed on every habitable continent on the planet, and unfortunately, slavery still goes on today in various forms. What made the children of Israel so special? Answering that they are God's chosen people only begs the question. *Chosen for what?* We know that God used the nation of Israel as an example to other nations of the world, but this suggests that God had something specific in mind when He chose them.

In turn, there had to be a reason why He so desired their freedom. If you read Exodus carefully, you will notice the repetition of one particular idea. Repeatedly, God used Moses to instruct Pharaoh to release the Israelites so that they may go worship Him. Over and over again, we read these words, and I'm inclined to believe that is precisely why God freed the children of Israel. It wasn't just so that they would be free. Rather, it was so that they would worship God and have a personal relationship with Him.

I would hope to God that we see the validity of this statement in our own lives, for God doesn't merely free someone for the concept of freedom. As a human being, to be free from something or someone is to be a servant to something or someone else because we were created to serve in love. In essence, we all worship something. And if you're going to worship anything, it might as well be the one person worthy of worship: God! God brings us out of slavery to ourselves, our sins, our proclivities, and our addictions so that we would go worship him instead of what previously mastered us.

From the slavery of the Hebrews under the Egyptians to the slavery of African Americans at the hands of European traders—and even those individuals who have endured human trafficking today, I am of the opinion that God brings you out of what held you so that you would be brought into the arms of the One who loves you. Whatever the Master brings you out of is a womb that held you in another world. However, when that womb opens, worship always erupts and ministry begins. With this in mind, we have a better understanding of Paul's words when he says, "It is for freedom that Christ has set us free. Stand firm, then, and do not let yourselves be burdened again by a yoke of slavery" (Gal. 5:1).

In the eyes of God, He is not *freeing us from*; He is making us *free to*. Free to what? Free to worship Him and be in relationship with Him. God frees the children of Israel on a spectacular level—a level that has prompted the production of films with Academy Award–winning special effects and singing of songs that barely hint at what the actual miraculous delivery must have been like. So powerfully did God free Israel from bondage that Miriam grabbed a tambourine and began to beat it to the glory of God, because those who once oppressed her and her kinsmen were drowned and never to be heard from again.

In the eyes of God, He is not freeing us from;
He is making us free to.

But this was only part of the equation. We have the freedom from bondage, but where did the worship and relationship come into play? I believe we see this in God's movement with the children of Israel as they wandered around the wilderness for forty years. He not only moved with them—God wooed them!

Wooed by the Husbandman

When was the last time you went out on a date? I'm not talking about simply meeting up with someone new. I speak of going all out and setting the stage for an experience with and for the one you love—creating a moment they will never forget. I don't ask in order to foster feelings of embarrassment for those who haven't dated in some time, and neither am I asking to further vaunt feelings of accomplishment for those who have. My question highlights the reason behind dating.

Though our contemporary society has changed what it means to date someone, the impetus behind dating and courting an individual is to woo them. When viewed in that light, the wooer calls out the one he or she is pursuing, the one he or she wants to love and to whom he or she wishes to show him- or herself. Remember the value we discovered in being alone and how the Master delivered Israel out of the hands of its oppressor? From there, Israel goes directly to the wilderness, and God's design for them was that they worship Him and come into relationship with Him. God did this with His mighty arm and, then, showed even more of Himself to them.

He fed them bread and quail directly from His table while giving them water from His rock, effectively treating His people to a five-star dinner. All of this happened as He cooled Israel during the day with His cloud that guided them and His romantic fire that warmed them at night. God *dated* Israel in the wilderness, showing them a scant amount of His capabilities in loving them every day. And, when He wanted to be close to them, God gave them the specifications of the setting in which He would meet them: El Moed, the tent of meeting, or Moses' tabernacle.

The tent of meeting was portable and would move with the entire camp. There, sacrifices would be offered up by the priests on a daily basis, and the high priest would enter the most holy place of the tent once a year on Israel's behalf. You may recall from chapter 6 how we looked at the specific instructions God gave for the construction of this place, but please also understand that the forty years of Israel's wandering in the wilderness was more than a form of punishment for their unbelief in their Deliverer-God, which Scripture points out (Num. 14:34).

Yes, Israel's unbelief doomed them to wander a year for every day they were allowed to examine the vastness and beauty of the blessed Promised Land God had sworn to give them. But consider what led God to call Abraham His friend—the fact that Abraham believed God. If Abraham's belief in God caused God to want to enter into a covenant relationship with Him, then Israel's wandering in the wilderness because of their unbelief wasn't something God issued simply because He likes torturing people. Proverbs reminds us of a greater motive: "For whom the LORD loves He corrects, Even as a father *corrects* the son in whom He delights" (Prov. 3:12 AMP).

Proverbs reminds us of a greater motive: "For whom the LORD loves He corrects, Even as a father corrects the son in whom He delights" (Prov. 3:12 AMP).

Bearing the Brokenness

If God corrects those He loves, I offer that Israel's wandering in the wilderness wasn't just because He was angry with them. Their wandering was because He was attempting to correct something that had gone wrong. Therefore, His continuous moving with them in the wilderness was because He wanted time to get out of them what their years of being slaves had put in them. And the best way to show anyone who you really are is to constantly be in their presence. We cannot flippantly gloss over this point, because it speaks directly to the situations and predicaments we encounter in our lives.

You may recall that the nation of Israel arrived in Egypt as a family of seventy people. While in Egypt for four hundred years, the children of Israel increased in number to a threatening degree to the Egyptians who called themselves the masters over Israel. During that time, though the children of Israel continued with their tradition of circumcision, it would only be a matter of common sense to understand that plenty of Egyptian customs and approaches to life got into the hearts and minds of Israel.

Four centuries—four hundred years—is an awfully long time. It's plenty of time to lose identity. Plenty of time to fall in love with different kinds of foods. Plenty of time to begin appreciating new varieties of music and other art forms. Plenty of time to learn to speak other languages and all their dialects. For nearly half a millennium, the children of Israel were soaking up Egyptian traditions, philosophies, and ways of life. We cannot ignore the fact that Israel began to identify itself with its oppressors, because that is precisely what abused, downtrodden, and exploited people do when left in a negative environment long enough.

There is a phrase used in the field of psychology that speaks to how people begin to fall in love and appreciate their captors and abusers. It's called Stockholm syndrome, and it develops between the abused and the abuser after they have spent time together. Though we have words to identify the phenomenon, it is still one of the most confusing anomalies I've ever encountered.

I recall one of the first instances in which I was counseling a woman suffering spousal abuse. To see the visceral damage her husband had done to her was so appalling that I had to control myself, lest I get physically involved in doing to him what he did to her. If you cannot tell, I am totally against any kind of abuse. And, I mean any. But as this woman sat in my office and informed my wife and me of everything her husband did to her, I was completely caught off guard when she began to speak so well of her husband and actually defend his actions. To hear her describe him would have you believing that she was speaking of a completely different person. My wife saw the bewilderment flood across my face, and when I opened my mouth to speak, her gentle hand rested on my arm to silence me. Later, Serita informed me of what goes on in the minds of abused women and victims of abuse because of her extensive dealings with the matter in her personal ministry sessions with other women.

Now, if such a thing could happen with a woman who was married to a man for a small number of years in comparison with the four hundred years Israel spent in Egypt, doesn't it make sense that something similar and worse could have happened to the children of Israel during their enslavement? In no way am I suggesting that the Jews loved the Egyptians' methods of oppression and maltreatment. What I am attempting to point out to you is that a person forgets parts of themselves in their misery because they are so wrapped up in trying to survive the relentless onslaught they are suffering. Having been distanced from their proper identity, they grab hold of what is nearby in their desperate need to be anchored by something even slightly recognizable. Unfortunately, their broken narrative has become palatable and, thereby, acceptable.

I'm quite sure you know exactly what I am talking about. You've been down so long that you have promised yourself that you would never hope again. You've made up in your mind that you won't dream again, and that you won't believe God again, because you fear your heart being torn to pieces just like it was the last time it crossed your mind to anticipate and wish for something better. Your adversity has been with you for so long that you have begun to identify yourself by your pain and consider your dysfunction and distress as normal.

But is that the life to which God has called any of us? If you believe that it is, I wholeheartedly yell at you with the authority of the Holy Spirit: *The devil is a liar!* God never intended for your temporary to be your eternity.

God never intended for your temporary to be your eternity.

Spiritual Fermentation

As God did with Israel, He is calling you out of the land of your oppression, your addiction, your pain, and the circumstances that have you believing that you will never get back up again. He has opened the door for you to begin your exodus, but you must put every ounce of your faith and trust in Him to do only what He can do, which is take care of you. He is calling you out so that you might worship Him and so that He might be given the opportunity to develop a relationship with you outside the purview of your abusers and your deadly habits. And, though He has called you to be with Him in the wilderness and witness how much He loves you, I will not ignore the overwhelming feeling that many experience when they are freed from any oppression.

They experience the sensation of being disoriented in the midst of their straggling.

We wander because we long for the days of familiarity, even when those days brought to us horrendous moments of pain, anguish, and a complete lack of hope. Because the first thing a person does when they are brought into a new space is to begin seeking out a way to stabilize themselves in the unfamiliar. Seeing that they can find no recognizable handle to hold onto in a new season, they look backward to something commonplace in order to receive comfort. For many, their comfort is pornography, even when it caused the end of their marriage. For others, it's alcohol abuse, though their liver is so hard and kidneys so shriveled that they've found themselves on a transplant list.

For some, it's the warmth of the arms of a previous lover, even though the hands attached to those arms have left marks and bruises on their faces that have caused them to lie in order to feebly attempt to explain away their existence. The familiarity for which many of us search can come in any form, and you would be surprised at what people do just to put themselves at ease during their season of wandering—that season when you look to something else in place of the God that freed you because even your Deliverer looks so strange to you that you would opt for destruction. After all, you're unable to tell the difference between the safe harbor of his presence and the rocky shores of destitution.

The coping mechanisms you've employed during your wandering have caused you to become spatially disoriented.

Like we see in the lives of the children of Israel and those who have suffered at the hands of abusers, could it be that our real problem of unbelief stems from the reality that we have put more of our faith in what and who has traumatized us than we have in the God who loves us? Is it possible, then, that our wandering because of our disbelief in the truth of God is a tool the Master uses to get "Egypt" out of us?

I ask these questions because of my experience in helping former drug addicts beat their chemical dependency. It is far easier to remove their attachment to the substance than it is to destroy their sociological dependence on it. Once an addict is out from under the influence of the drug, their counselor must set about correcting the environment and severing the person's attachment to their surroundings that led the addict to seek the substance in the first place. So, I ask my previous questions another way: Could God's proclamation of Israel's wandering be the next step in the process of Israel's exodus from Egypt, but centering on the more important aspect of finally removing Israel's connection to their history of abuse?

In traveling with Israel throughout their forty years in the wilderness, God was impressing upon His people their need to form a connection with someone who loved them instead of holding onto the relationship with those who had enslaved them. But when we look at this thought through the lens of being crushed, I begin to see some similarities. At each stage—seeding, sprouting, fruiting, harvest, crushing, and transformation into wine—we are continuously beckoned to forget what we previously were through our death to one aspect and entrance into another, or higher, form. And, throughout every transformation, the Husbandman was present, just like He was with Israel in the wilderness. Wherever God's cloud went, they went with Him. In the midst of them was the tent of meeting because God sought to tabernacle with and live among His people.

Wherever God's cloud went, they went with Him.

What if the final stage of the crushing process is meant to ensure an eternal cohabitation between God and His people, both of them being forever reconnected? What if having God inside us is the agent of spiritual fermentation needed to transform us into wine?

The Indwelling Wine

We have been called out of our bondage to be brought into a relationship with God. After all, the principal reason behind Jesus' death, burial, and resurrection was our reconnection back to God. When Christ was crushed on our behalf, He took for us the eternal ramifications of our existence apart from God's presence and power. Having bridged that gap between our temporal nature and God's eternal nature, God and humanity are now able to not only coexist, but also have a relationship with one another. Let us not forget the simple reason behind all of God's plan: *He's putting His family back together!*

God was healing His marriage with His people.

What sense does it make to be next to your bride, however, and be unable to be intimate with your bride? How can you be intimate with that you do not touch? Though God met with His people at the tent of meeting, it only makes sense that He would want to touch His people. For that is how humanity previously existed with God. God was Adam's source of life and power. It was Adam's transgression that led to humanity's total disconnection from God. Therefore, God's aim has been to reclaim within the heart of every human being the place in which He rightfully resides as source. Instead of our will and limited knowledge being the failing battery that we would use to power our lives, God wishes to be the endless source of life in the core of who we are.

God's aim has been to reclaim within the heart of every human being the place in which He rightfully resides as source.

So, you see, coming close to us via the tent of meeting was not enough for the Husbandman. He desires more than proximity; the Master craves His eternal reality of intimacy. Instead of residing close by, God's motive is to inhabit. And He has done everything to implement that by giving us the gift of His Holy Spirit. We're told, "Suddenly a sound like the blowing of a violent wind came from heaven and filled the whole house where they were sitting. They saw what seemed to be tongues of fire that separated and came to rest on each of them. All of them were filled with the Holy Spirit and began to speak in other tongues as the Spirit enabled them" (Acts 2:2–4).

Other than the day of Jesus' birth and His latter days of death, burial, and resurrection, there is no other day more important to the New Testament saint than the day of Pentecost. This day was fifty days after the Passover celebration, and we've already discussed the significance behind that celebration. However, the day of Pentecost holds a special place in the heart of the Christian because it is the day God introduced the world to the Holy Spirit. To some, this occasion might mean nothing, but we get a better understanding of the gravity of this event when we consider the previous interactions the Holy Spirit had with humanity.

All throughout the Old Testament, we read about

instances of how the Holy Spirit "came upon" Moses and others. You would read how the Holy Spirit "came upon" David, how the Holy Spirit "came upon" Samson, or how the Holy Spirit "came upon" Gideon. During these moments, the men the Holy Spirit "came upon" were able to accomplish supernatural feats all to the glory of God. Nevertheless, as wonderful as each of these occurrences were, you will notice that the influence of the Holy Spirit upon these people was temporary. It is not until you get to the day of Pentecost as described in the second chapter of Acts that you see a different word used to detail the actions of the Holy Spirit.

It's then that we see the Holy Spirit *fill* and *rest upon* someone.

The Holy Spirit is no longer paying brief, momentary visits. No, instead He is permanently taking up residence and indwelling His people. So new was this constant habitation of the Holy Spirit that it made the remaining disciples' passersby believe the lie that Peter and his cohorts had indulged in too much wine.

On the day of Pentecost, God had effectively moved from dwelling close to His people in the tabernacle and being with His people via Christ to living in His people by the Holy Spirit. But in the Old Testament, we see God moving with the children of Israel in the wilderness during their wandering as He began purging them of the stain of their oppression. In the New Testament, we see God walking among His people and informing them of the reality of the Kingdom of Heaven being at hand through Christ. But on the day of Pentecost, God takes up residence in His people, and we see Him doing perfectly the very same thing we saw Him doing when we met Him in Genesis—moving!

The Master moves with us today because He is in us, indwelling in our hearts and guiding us. Gone are the days when God's people sought the priests for a word from Him. Gone are the days when you had to venture to the tabernacle to be near Him. Gone are the days when you had to press through the crowd and touch the hem of Christ's garment to be healed. Gone are the days when you had to sit among a crowd of five thousand just to hear Him. Gone are the days when Jesus had to visit the tomb of your loved one so that they would be resurrected.

The Master moves with us today because He is in us, indwelling in our hearts and guiding us.

At this moment, you live in a day and age when the mere presence of the Holy Spirit removes cancer from the body, heals people of HIV/AIDS, reunites families by the changing of unforgiving hearts, resurrects the dead, and restores the dreams you had given up on long ago. The contemporary possibility of those miracles that were wrought because of the Holy Spirit "coming upon" someone or Jesus physically interacting with someone or something have been exponentially increased because the Master is no longer confined to a tent of meeting in the wilderness or one physical body.

God now indwells the hearts of the hundreds of millions of people all across this planet who have placed their hopes and faith solely in Him. Instead of there being one temple, every believer is a temple in which He meets with them and to which every person seeking a relationship with God can visit and become one whom He indwells.

God's divine mobility has always been at work, and it has been His desire that we become part of it and get in on the action. The indwelling of the wine of His Holy Spirit on the inside of us is merely the final stage of His personal crushing that He endured for humanity. When you allow God's Spirit to dwell in you, you can know without a doubt that He is at work in your life—in the dark and dirty places, in the hard and painful places, and in the power and presence required to see real change in your life. Simply put, my friend, your spiritual fermentation is at hand!

CHAPTER 12

An Eternal Pairing

That is what mortals misunderstand. They say of some temporal suffering, "No future bliss can make up for it," not knowing that Heaven, once attained, will work backwards and turn even that agony into a glory.

—*C. S. Lewis*

I remember one of the first times my wife and I tasted a great wine. It was untold years ago, and I had made a reservation and took Serita out for a romantic dinner at a new restaurant we wanted to try. The waiter introduced himself, told us about the various specialties for which the restaurant was known, handed us the menus, and gave us a wine list. After perusing the menu and choosing our courses, the waiter revisited us and complimented us on our choices. Before I could even tell him the wine we chose, he politely chimed in his personal suggestion—a cabernet sauvignon that was, at that time, older than two of my children.

He began describing why it was the best choice and how it would bring out the more subtle flavors of the food we had ordered that evening. This gentleman knew how to make it sound like the perfect wine for our perfect meal. He could have been selling us a bottle of Welch's grape juice, and we would have gone for it simply because of how he described the flavors. We agreed and I did something I rarely do—I did *not* look at the price.

Upon sniffing and sampling it, however, we could see the inspiration for his enthusiasm. He poured us a couple of glasses and left the bottle. As Serita and I began discussing our selections, the waiter and another server showed up with our first course. As the server transferred our food from his tray to the table, the waiter told us more about the wine, the vineyard that produced it, and wine from that region of Italy.

Finally, we each took a bite and followed it with a sip. Amazing! The consummation of flavors from the marriage of the food and wine transcended our imagination. How could that cabernet so perfectly complement the tastes on our palate?

No Good Reason

We knew there were guidelines to pairing wine with food, but experiencing it that night showed us what all the fuss was about. Generally, you learn that red wines pair best with bolder-flavored red meats and savory dishes while white wines go well with fish, seafood, and chicken. You want a wine that complements and even enhances the food while possessing its own intensity and flavor.

These suggestions are time-honored traditions because great chefs and winemakers throughout history have explored the relationship between fine wine and good food. For thousands of years, people have enjoyed their meals with a chosen wine because, together with their meal, it accentuates the subtle flavors of foods and makes dining a more delightful experience. As a result, food and wine are a timeless pair.

Our meal that night lasted several hours and included several courses, but there's another timeless pairing that lasts much longer. In fact, it's eternal: the relationship between you and the Master. Your relationship with God exhausts the length of all time because an eternal God cannot produce anything less than an eternal seed. Therefore, each of us is intended for the ever after. We are eternal spirits temporarily in earthly bodies.

Your relationship with God exhausts the length of all time because an eternal God cannot produce anything less than an eternal seed.

You and God have been locked into a timeless relationship that only paused when you were born into the earth. Eternity past and eternity future are separated only by the slender sliver of time in which you and I now exist in this lifetime on earth. Before time began, you were with God, and when time ends, you will be with Him again. Simply put, you and God were meant for each other.

It's the agony that lies within the brevity of time that makes us doubt Him and His plan. Unfortunately, we allow our limited understanding of pain to drive us into the arms of temporary idols that will never be able to appreciate the eternal vintage that makes us so unique. All too often, instead of running to the Master Vintner, we heed the call of sex, drugs, money, or whatever else we believe will drown out the still, small voice of the Lover of our souls as He beckons for us through His use of the discomfort we hate so much.

The truth is that we've all cheated on Him from time to time.

You tried to do your own thing. You fought to go your own way. Even still, because of the root of faith that was deep inside, you ultimately had to turn around, return home to His arms, bow yourself before Him, and realize that all you've ever gotten in your life comes from your Father. Yes, you might have the proclivities to serve the devil—we all have the sinful human nature of our original parents, Adam and Eve—but deeper than that lies a commitment to the Lord, because there's something about loving God that lingers.

No matter how hard you might try, you can't escape the spiritual bond between you and your Maker. You can't drink it away. You can't smoke it away. You can't sex it away. You can attempt to walk away from God and live your life as you see fit, but the Master has placed a hook in you that prevents you from doing anything that would spoil the future wine He is laboring to produce in you. In other words, He remains faithful even when we don't.

Despite our attempts to escape our crushing, God is intent on converting us from one level of life to another one. What He is doing with you is not built on your finished work. Your salvation and new identity are built on the finished work of Christ, and that finished work was done with everlasting effect just as He is God forever. As we have seen, we can look throughout all the Old Testament until now and see the Master's blood-red wine seeping out of eternity and into this present moment.

Despite our attempts to escape our crushing, God is intent on converting us from one level of life to another one.

What would prompt an eternal God to trade His splendor in heaven for the dullness of earth, compel Him to wrap Himself in flesh, and motivate Him to become like His creation? What would cause the Almighty, the Creator of heaven and earth, to forsake the eternal and become temporal? Why would an omnipotent God strip Himself of His power, venture to earth, and become as weak as we are?

There's no good reason—there's only the perfect reason known as God's love. Driven by His love for us and knowing that we were powerless to transform and save ourselves, the Master stepped in as our substitute. Instead of requiring us to blindly endure the trampling of our lives without a vision of what we would become, Jesus set the prime example by going first and allowing His crushed body to be lifted up on the cross for all to see.

Christ showed us His wine so that we might be enticed by the production of ours.

If the Master is eternal and has redeemed us forever, however, we should see something being crushed on our behalf and lifted up even in our pasts. We should be able to see God working to prepare His people in order that He may be paired with them as an example of what can happen when we are together once again. If the Master's blood has been spilled on our behalf and smeared throughout time, He obviously wants to be paired again with all of humanity. A brief look at God's divine wine list confirms this truth.

Holy Hide-and-Seek

God has promised that we will find Him if we seek Him (Jer. 29:13). From all my years of actively pursuing God, though, I've discovered that He loves to play hide-and-seek. He doesn't always hide in the most obvious places, but He leaves a trail of spiritual bread crumbs for us to follow when He's chosen an out-of-the-way place in which to conceal Himself. God is easily spotted during our joyous seasons, but it often seems as if he's an expert at tucking Himself away in the most obscure locations during our trying times.

Could it be, however, that God hasn't hidden Himself during our tumultuous seasons, but rather He has simply revealed Himself in a form we've yet to recognize? After all, even the disciples at first believed Jesus was a ghost when they saw Him walking on the wind-tossed sea. No wonder then, that they demanded to see Him for themselves after He arose from the tomb. They couldn't grasp how Christ could so dramatically change the course of nature as they understood it and still be the Master they knew and loved.

Before we criticize their reluctance to recognize Him, we might look first at our own ability to spot God in our lives. Tell me, can you recognize God in another form, or must He always reveal Himself to you through the construct of your familiarity?

You and I are not the first ones to struggle with glimpsing God's presence, nor were the disciples. Moses and the Israelites experienced such a test while out in the wilderness. In the Old Testament in Numbers 21, we see a nation concerned about their provision while grappling with a disbelief that led them to verbalize their disdain for the Lord and His servant, Moses.

It wasn't just the murmuring and complaining

that provoked God to wrath; it was the unbelief in their hearts that brought on God's swift correction. If there's anything that God has always requested His people to do, it is believe Him. For how can you seek or worship a God you do not trust?

If there's anything that God has always requested His people to do, it is believe Him.

Israel had every reason to believe God. The Lord had brought them out of Egypt with a mighty hand. First, God crippled and destroyed Egypt with ten deadly plagues. When Pharaoh decided that he would not let Israel go, the Almighty then lured him and his army into the Red Sea, where they drowned. Surely, the extent to which the Master went to rescue Israel was also a sign that He wouldn't simply lead them into the desert just to let them perish. If God wanted the children of Israel dead, He could have let them die at the hands of Pharaoh.

It's the same with us. The Vinedresser wouldn't have gone to all of the trouble to develop us if He was going to destroy us. If the Lord wanted us dead, He could have killed us before we ever brought forth fruit.

Yet, in the face of such evidence, the Hebrews believed

their fear instead of trusting God. Doesn't that sound familiar? I cannot be the only one plagued with panic during the afflictions of life. When faced with calamities, we believe our fears of destruction and forget that God is present, even though He may be hiding from our physical senses. But a hidden God does not equal an absent God. Like a grape transformed into wine, God is training us to recognize Him in another form.

God didn't allow His people to die after delivering them from Egypt. As they wandered in the desert, suddenly the population began thinning out because they were being bitten by poisonous snakes. Instantly, God gave Moses instructions to beat brass into the shape of a serpent and wrap it around a staff. Then, he was to lift up the staff so that everyone bitten could look upon it and be healed.

Fast-forward several centuries, and we see God showing up in the form of Christ upheld on the cross so that you and I could be healed. Tried in a furnace and beaten into the form of what had bitten the children of Israel, the staff was a precursor to the cross of our salvation. What Moses did to the brass was a sign of what Jesus would endure via the crucifixion. God could have given instructions to Moses to have the brass shaped into anything else, so why would the Lord require Moses to beat brass into the shape of the very thing that bit Israel?

You can only redeem what is kin to you.

Foreshadowing the step Christ would take with us, God showed up in a different form. He revealed that He would become like those He intended to save and those He desired to be paired with once again. Finally, in the life and death and new life of Christ, we see God coming as one of us to save and transform us. In essence, the eternal wine of the Father—His Son, Jesus—became a lowly grape like us to show all grapes that we could become eternal wine like Him.

Sometimes, however, our transformation seems delayed. We can't make sense of the detours and derailments that send us through the desert instead of along a straight course to our destination. But what if some of what we call distractions are actually divine forms of guidance? Could it be possible that God is also showing His hand in unfamiliar methods? Where we are accustomed to God directing us in manners we're comfortable with, He steps outside the box and employs something altogether different, yet effective.

Where we are accustomed to God directing us in manners we're comfortable with, He steps outside the box and employs something altogether different, yet effective.

Spiritual ADD

After all, God has to keep our attention. Just like the children of Israel, we're prone to spiritual attention deficit disorder. We want to trust Him and move through our crushing and fermenting and become His holy wine, but we struggle to wait, to hope, to remain faithful even as He remains faithful.

Have you ever desired something for so long that you resolved in yourself that it was never going to happen? Have you ever had to declare that your dreams were dead so that you would finally have a moment's peace? It's the delay in the fulfillment of the promises of God that cause us so much pain. When the Master gives us the vision of what he's going to do in our lives, He shows us the mountain peaks while He hides the valleys. If you saw the climb you would have to endure to get to the mountaintop, you would abandon the entire trip.

It's the passion we have for the fulfillment of God's promise that drives us, but it's the play between the pain and passion that He uses to refine us. It's our passions we have to make peace with when we are confronted with the delayed realization of God's promises because passion makes you dissatisfied with what you have as you wait for what you want. In the face of waiting to be paired again with God, we fight with putting our hopes to bed in order that we might deal with the agony of delay. So we cry our dreams to sleep because it's easier for us to allow our passions to rest instead of allowing them to remain and go unfulfilled.

But the Master is not in the business of torturing His children through delays. Rather it's the hidden things in the valleys of "not yet" and "wait" that make us who we are. God gets our attention with the hidden things that lie in wait in the valleys—the things that happen that we didn't see coming or expect.

It's the problems that catch us off guard that are so alarming and amazing. During those times you have to decide how you're going to react to what happens to you because you can't control what life throws your way. But you do have a choice in how you will respond. Do you give up on God, put your dreams to the side, and make up in your mind that the promises of God will never come to pass?

Or do you trust the One that holds you even though the valleys of life threaten to claim your faith as their next casualty?

If God uses our valleys to prepare us for the peaks, we must realize that we are not yet ready for the promises that reside at such a great height. After all, God hides His treasures until we can handle them.

And since we can't see the value of what's coming, we don't look for the incredible. It's while we're not looking that things are moving. It's while we're sleeping in the valleys that God does His best work because the Master does not need our help as He transforms us. He requires only our faith and humility.

I am thoroughly convinced that God made me who I am in the low places of my life. It's the nights that I cried myself to sleep and my tears crawled across the bridge of my nose that God most often used to develop me into the person I am today. It was the hidden things in the valleys that God used to kill off my fleshly desires and strip from me everything that would prevent me from being His wine. I had to learn not to fear my valley experiences but accept them—and that process continues. And I believe you must do the same.

I am thoroughly convinced that God made me who I am in the low places of my life.

Think for a moment about your natural defenses. What do you do when you're confronted with the things you never saw coming? How do you handle slipping into valley experiences? What happens when all the snakes seem to bite at once? All was going well, but then your foot slipped and the house is gone. Or one minute you were walking along together, and then a snake appeared and your marriage is over.

Your foot slipped, and now the kids aren't talking to you. A snake bites you and now you've been fired. Suddenly there's another one, and now you've lost a loved one. It's through the crushing power of the valleys that we are transformed. So often we don't need the Master to teach us how to handle the peaks of blessings as much as we need Him to show us how to handle the valleys of preparation. We don't currently need the lesson of how to handle the wine; we need the Master to teach us how to handle the crushing.

We know God's going to do something, but we don't know when. We know God is going to bless us, but we don't know how. We know God is going to connect us, but we don't know through whom. God told you He was going to deliver you, but He didn't tell you what He was going to deliver you from. God said you'd be together with Him again, but He didn't tell you everything you'd endure along the way.

All of this is preparation for your final pairing with the Master. You're doing everything to avoid the hidden crushings in the valleys, but those are what's needed to bring you to the point of being reunited and paired with God. Don't get lost by the distractions.

Prepared for Resurrection

The trauma and pain God has ordered in your life has exposed the dreams you've put to the side and allowed to die. It's the crushing you experience in the low parts of your life, however, that God will use as His resurrection tools to bring them back to life. What's going on with you is God's job. There is something dead in your house, and He seeks to revive it. Are you tired of the deathly stench of your deceased dreams? Are you tired of looking good but not feeling good? Are you tired of smiling but not having joy?

The finished product you see on the peaks is the end result of the resurrection in the valley.

The finished product you see on the peaks is the end result of the resurrection in the valley.

Just like Jesus experienced the turmoil, pain, and depression in the low parts of His life before His transformation, we will experience the same. If we were meant to reunite with Him in eternity, we must make the same journey through the valleys of preparation that He did. You didn't simply tumble into trauma. You were led into it, escorted into it by the Master Vintner who so wants to be with you that He said, "Look. I'll go first. I'll endure the crushing to become wine."

The blessings and transformation we've sought for so long have been promised to us by a God who did not free us from bondage just to be destroyed in the deserts and valleys of unbelief and unfulfilled longings. Do not retreat back to the familiar caves of abandoned hopes and deceased dreams. The eternal pairing we once enjoyed with the Father is coming in short order. And though you may be crying, "Don't make me hope again," the Master is showing Himself to you in a different and newer form that is proof that none of what you experienced is in vain. Even your delays are fitting into His plan to prepare you.

The new form God has taken is the one you will one day assume for your pairing when you and He are finally together for all eternity. Your wine will last for all of time. Don't sacrifice the quality because you can't see beyond your pain. Trust Him. He knows exactly—*exactly*—what it's like to endure the crushing you've been through. God is committed to you through it all and beyond. Your pairing with Him knows no end.

CHAPTER 13

A Tasting with the King

The heart, like the grape, is prone to delivering its harvest in the same moment that it appears to be crushed.

—*Roger Housden*

Wine tastings have become a popular social event. Most tastings limit the number of guests to fit the intimate, casual atmosphere of the host and their setting. Some locales boast a rustic ambience with the sampling conducted outdoors or on a terrace or patio. Others brandish a trendier vibe in sleek, minimalist restaurants or state-of-the-art wine cellars.

The atmosphere and style might vary, but most

wine tastings follow a similar pattern. After a certain number of guests arrive, the host welcomes everyone and the tasting begins. The sommelier, or wine steward, leads the flavorful experience, usually explaining the vintage and composition of the wines to be sampled. Many of these experts delve into the processes employed by vintners to produce their particular vintages and types of wine. Wine tastings facilitate conversation among guests, a true group experience, while allowing them to each enjoy their individual sips of the festivity's offerings.

While wine tastings sound pleasant enough, I can't help but notice how different they seem compared to the rambunctious parties, elaborate feasts, and dramatic festivals held in ancient Israel during harvest seasons. These events were celebratory in nature, each of them representing a moment of Jewish history when God had done something miraculous on behalf of His children.

By Royal Invitation

Because Israel, during its antiquity, was an agrarian society, harvests indicated tangibly how God had kept His promises to provide for His people. The children of Israel annually celebrated seven different feasts: the

Feast of Passover, the Feast of Unleavened Bread, the Feast of Firstfruits, the Feast of Weeks (Pentecost), the Feast of Trumpets (Rosh Hashanah), the Day of Atonement (Yom Kippur), and the Feast of Tabernacles. Even as these seven feasts commemorated something God had done for Israel, I find it extremely difficult to believe that they would not include the production of new wine as part of their celebration.

Harvests indicated tangibly how God had kept His promises to provide for His people.

I suspect Israel celebrated God's fulfillment of His promises to them at least seven times during the year because it doesn't take much to burst into spontaneous praise of the Master. From my own experience, all I have to do is remember the times when I had no electricity or running water in the house— those times when I just *knew* that it was the end for me and my family. It was then when I'd find myself standing with lifted hands, singing a song of spontaneous praise, or crying with tears running down my face. If you caught me at the right moment, you probably would have seen all three!

I wonder, though, if Israel was celebrating God's

work on their behalf, could it be possible that God was celebrating *them* at the same time? It makes plenty of sense when you place all of this into the context of a parent who celebrates the achievements of their child, or when they give a child a gift and see the smile on their face. The random giving of any gift to someone you love "just because" causes the receiver to erupt into laughter, cries, and the giving of many thanks. The giver receives joy in return because they were doing nothing but expressing their love.

Jesus' parable about the talents or bags of gold that the master entrusts to his servants while he is away (Matt. 25:14-30) teaches us that He will give more to those who have plenty, and I now understand why. The receipt, appreciation, and proper use of his investment in us builds confidence that He can trust us with more. Hasn't that been true of your experience? When you give something to a child and they do well with it, are you not inspired to give in increasing measure?

If the Master Vintner was celebrating Israel while Israel was celebrating Him, then I believe He throws the most lavish party in response to you becoming what He has labored for you to become. There seems to be a role reversal in this process. Instead of you laboring to yield a harvest, the Husbandman did all the work in cultivating you. Upon harvesting you, He began crushing and fermenting you so that you would be more.

As you move beyond your crushing and fermenting, God then begins setting the table, and this will not be a normal wine tasting done on a Saturday evening with a group of friends. The Master is celebrating you, the completion of the labor He has performed in you, and the investment He has placed within you. The festival He is throwing in response to us becoming wine will be boisterous and noisy, spirited and lively. It will be a celebration filled with immense joy, because God's presence cannot be filled with anything less than complete awe, peace, security, purpose, righteousness, and worship.

The Master hasn't invited us to an average tasting like we might enjoy at a friend's house. Instead He invites us to a feast that puts all others to shame. In no shape, form, or fashion will this feast take place in a trendy setting that received a few five-star online reviews. The Master Vintner has spared no expense in procuring for His feast in an upper room the likes of which we have never seen. The Lord has invited us to His mercy seat in an all new Most Holy Place that we see in Solomon's tabernacle.

Righteous RSVP

Only those who are in covenant with the Lord, those who are righteous by the blood of Jesus Christ, may RSVP to the invitation to meet with Him behind the veil. Traveling beyond the inner court and arriving in the Holiest of Holies, you have direct access to the King of All Creation. His unrestrained presence resides there, and He requests that you bring only yourself—the precious wine He labored so hard to produce. Before He releases such a priceless vintage to the rest of the world, it would only make sense that the Master Vintner be able to enjoy a cask unto Himself.

This is the beckoning of an eternal God who anticipates the arrival of one He so dearly loves. You, His fruit, having descended into the depths like Christ after being crushed, experienced the Inner Court fermentation. Now, however, that grape no longer exists. Something else has taken its place. The grape is now wine, having risen with new life in a new form like Christ. As a result, the veil that has always stood between the Vintner and the grapes no longer exists between the King and His wine.

---

*The veil that has always stood between the Vintner
and the grapes no longer exists between the King
and His wine.*

The Glory of the Lord was waiting on *you*. The holding pattern into which the Ark of the Covenant was locked was not only because of the actions of sinful men, but because the Lord had found someone through whom He would later set up a home where He would receive invited guests. David's tabernacle, like Christ's time in the tomb and our time in fermentation, was temporary. Something permanent and eternal beckons us on to a greater level of life. A new realm has opened up to us that makes our reality, with its outer court and inner court experiences, look like the shadow it really is.

If our analogy of Christ's death, burial, and resurrection aligns with the tabernacle and its parts, there must be a third temple that represents the eternal nature of our resurrected and risen Christ, the wine He has made us out to be, and the endless communion we would have with the Master Vintner in His presence. And there is.

Only one compartment exists in all three Old

Testament iterations of the tabernacle that fit our requirements: the Holy of Holies, or Most Holy Place! Nowhere else in all three areas of the temple can we find the unrestrained presence of God as found enthroned between the cherubim on the mercy seat atop the Ark of the Covenant. Above all else, God's presence alone is what we seek.

In God's presence there is eternal life in which we exist as His wine. In His presence, we experience the intimacy and communion He sought to enjoy with us ever since the fall of man. In God's presence, we fully grasp who and what we truly are through the resurrection of Christ. In effect, the Master Vintner has carried us through an outer court crushing, an inner court refinement, and into a Holiest of Holies for eternity.

Holy House Party

The beauty of every ounce of wine we carry is contained by what our Lord Jesus did for us in the Most Holy Place. He was, in fact, the first to RSVP to God's eternal invitation:

> But when Christ appeared as a high priest of the good things that have come, then through

the greater and more perfect tent (not made with hands, that is, not of this creation) He entered once for all into the holy places, not by means of the blood of goats and calves but by means of His own blood, thus securing an eternal redemption. For if the blood of goats and bulls, and the sprinkling of defiled persons with the ashes of a heifer, sanctify for the purification of the flesh, how much more will the blood of Christ, who through the eternal Spirit offered Himself without blemish to God, purify our conscience from dead works to serve the living God. (Heb. 9:11–14 ESV)

Jesus did not arrive at the mercy seat through the temporary blood of animals. All at once, Jesus was both the sacrifice that was crushed and our High Priest. Therefore, the blood He sprinkled upon the mercy seat in the eternal tabernacle was His own and a foretaste of what we would become after He transformed us. In essence, Jesus brought His own wine to the intimate tasting at God's table.

And seeing that what the Vintner does in our lives is patterned directly after what happened in Christ's resurrection, the Vintner calls us to the secret chambers of His presence, too. It's with the Master that we finally see something we've not seen in the previous compartments of the tabernacle. We see that there is no more crushing, no more refinement or process, and no more struggle and strife. Instead, the process has been replaced by something altogether different. Instead of work, there is only relationship and being who we truly are—the wine of our King.

When it comes to what God has done in our lives, the transformation through which He has taken us, and what we are called to, it is important that we remove from our minds the stages of old. There is nothing wrong with remembering how the Father has carried you. However, we often have a penchant for clinging to the past at the expense of our futures. Now that we are wine, we cannot afford to continue thinking like grapes, remaining in the outer court and not pressing on to greater things.

Now that we are wine, we cannot afford to continue thinking like grapes.

As a result, the wine is brought to the last compartment of the tabernacle—the Most Holy Place. Here we step into the temple befitting the joy of God's final harvest festival. Here in this Most Holy Place the Vintner invites us to a private communion with

Him so that we might sample together what He has created in us along with His plans to share us with the world.

In this festival, it's not only a reuniting of our Father with His children, but also a modern coming together of the wine and bread in a celestial upper room experience reminiscent of what Jesus did in that Last Supper with His disciples. This is a holy house party like no other. It all comes full circle now: the symbolic parts and sacred pieces of the tabernacle in the Old Testament; the reality of the Incarnation as Jesus became human in order to suffer for our sins, die on the cross, and rise again; and the crushing you have experienced in your own life in order to become the precious, holy wine fit for a King.

This eternal nature that we carry within us directs us to the day that we will no longer need physical sustenance but will subsist only on the spiritual bread that Christ gave to His disciples in the upper room in the form of physical bread. If you remember, however, bread wasn't the only thing Jesus offered them. With that bread, He gave them wine, a symbol of the blood that was spilled on our behalf and placed on the mercy seat.

Through the crushing brokenness Christ endured, His blood became the new wine after which our transformation was patterned. We were destined to

291

become that same kind of wine by the same Vintner and His process of crushing us. In essence, then, the bread of life and wine of the spirit have beckoned us with glad hearts into God's presence so that we would enjoy a higher, better, and eternal communion with Him.

Only in this new communion, we find one special difference. Now there is intimacy, a give and a take between one another. Where the Master would give, we would receive. Now that we are like Him as His wine, we offer ourselves to Him so that He would delight in what we have become. There is no need for us to be bread, because His body serves as that for us.

Like the most excellent host, God supplied for us what we could not supply for ourselves. And because His supply is never depleted, we needn't worry about this feast ending soon. Seeing that the wine we embody is eternal and connected directly to Him we, too, will never run dry. Therefore, this festival will never end, but continue unhindered between the Master Vintner and His new cask of wine—his new creation.

Like the most excellent host, God supplied for us what we could not supply for ourselves.

Beyond Blessed

As we embrace being God's new creation in Christ, as we grow accustomed to living as His holy wine, then we begin experiencing new levels of joy, peace, contentment, purpose, and satisfaction. No longer do we wonder why we are here on this earth. We know that everything we have been through is more than worth it because God has used it all, wasting nothing, to bring us to the point in our lives where we are now.

Your crushing is not the end—it's only the beginning.

I'm far from perfect, but I have experienced the blessing of being holy wine to those around me. And lest you think I boast, please understand that what I'm called to do humbles me on a daily basis. There is no way I can do anything on my own. But through Christ, I can do all things.

There, I am beyond blessed to do what I do. There is nothing like seeing someone's life changed by the grace of God, and I'm overwhelmed that the Master would choose me to be even a small part in what he's doing here on earth. People have run up to me with tears in their eyes, unloaded their entire life's story in a matter of minutes, and told me how a message they heard changed the way they look at themselves and how they relate to God.

I've seen murderers repent at the foot of the cross and turn to others and begin praying with them. I've witnessed broken marriages being mended because the love of God was imprinted upon the hearts of two individuals who had sworn they would die hating each other. I've seen how the Holy Spirit has turned strippers into teachers, drug dealers into upstanding salesmen, and the most corrupt people you can imagine into deacons in the church and beacons of honesty. With God, nothing is impossible.

All of these people I've witnessed came from different backgrounds, but the common factor between each of them is the sanctifying blood-wine that was spilled that fateful day on Golgotha. Where they once had no hope of ever being granted an audience with the Holy God, all of that changed when they embraced Christ as their Lord and Savior. They went from being illegitimate to being heirs, from prodigal to passionate, and from hopeless to happiness. They have been sanctified all through the actions of someone else, Jesus Christ, who did the work for them. After all, one's crushing always gives rise to something wonderful in someone else's life. Jesus was the first and we now follow His example.

One's crushing always gives rise to something wonderful in someone else's life. Jesus was the first and we now follow His example.

At one fell swoop, each of these believers was transformed in the eyes of the Lord. Individuals facing desperate situations went from "Access Denied" to "Access Granted" in their relationship with God. That is what all of this is about.

Jesus took for us what we would never be able to handle on our own, but the Master was not content with just saving us. No! He wishes for us to be like Him so that we would be intimate and commune with Him. And, though He bore the punishment for all our transgressions and sin, He endeavored to take us through the process of preparing us for the face-to-face meeting we would have with the Father.

Hence, our crushing.

Having survived and thrived in the crushing and fermentation, though, we can now hear the heavy locks of the eternal doors to His presence release, because on the other side of the thick veil stands the Almighty God who wishes an audience with us even more than we do with Him. For during the conversation we would have with Him, our Father desires to partake of a vintage He has on His Son's authority is "a very good year"!

Wine for the World

No more process. No more delay. You have direct access.

Now that you have an unobstructed avenue into the Shekinah Presence of God, Himself, He begs that you sit with Him and pour Him a chalice of the wine you've brought with you.

You may struggle to see yourself as God's holy wine now, and that's understandable. But the truth of the matter is that you are not what and who you used to be. You are not what you did. You are not your lack. You are not what people have labeled you to be, and God will continue confronting you to make you understand who you are.

You are not a grape. You are not even the crushed hull and flesh that remains after being trampled. You are something far better. You are wine. When God sees you, He sees you as perfect. When God's eyes rest on you, He doesn't see who and what you used to be; instead He sees the fully developed you in Christ. He sees the righteous you. In the Bible we're told that we are the righteousness of God in Christ (2 Cor. 5:21) and that in this world we are as He is (1 John 4:17). God's Word tells the truth about who you are—so believe it!

God's Word tells the truth about who you are—so believe it!

I realize it can be challenging to accept the truth about who you are. If the Bible has been telling people the truth about themselves for thousands of years, you would think that people would have gotten the message by now. That would be the logical conclusion, but you would be completely taken aback by how arduous it is to get people to simply walk in what they believe. Just think about it. The ramifications of walking in the faith we profess are immense.

Addictions and perversions would be gone in a flash. Some people would lose over thirty pounds and have all types of diseases completely expelled from their bodies. You cannot afford to miss this point. Walking in the full measure of the faith doesn't mean you won't encounter problems and setbacks, but it does mean that you will eventually rise above them. Living your life in what Christ has done in and for you changes your entire existence because Jesus has already changed your entire existence!

Do you understand that Jesus has already done everything for you?

You must accept this truth because God is more than satisfied with the wine He has produced in you. He is elated with how you have turned out, keeping a cask unto Himself as a trophy proudly displayed in His personal winery. But He has a plan for the rest of your bottled vintage that entails you being offered to the world as a sign for what He wants to do with other grapes.

The Vintner wants others to taste the masterpiece He has produced in His new creation. You have His power within you. You have full access to all the riches in Christ. He wants you to offer hope to those being crushed and struggling to understand. He wants to work through you to comfort the desolate, heal the sick, strengthen the weak, and reveal the light of His love in a dim world.

You are God's trophy, and He wants to show you off.

CHAPTER 14

The Wedding Planner

This life is not godliness, but growth in godliness;
not health, but healing; not being, but becoming;
not rest, but exercise. We are not now what we
shall be, but we are on the way.

—Martin Luther

You wouldn't believe my mailbox in the preceding months before June each year. I'm inundated with wedding invitations! I'm honored that so many people would invite me to the celebration of their marital union, but I'm only one man. And with approximately 2.5 million weddings happening on average each year in our country, I simply can't make all of them.

Recently, however, while walking back from collecting my mail and sifting through the numerous decorative, crisp linen invitations that filled my mailbox, I was stopped in my tracks. Why would someone send me an invitation to their wedding? Obvious reasons came to mind. I understand that someone wants me to witness them taking their marriage vows. In other cases, I'm asked to officiate the wedding. I get that. But my question that day centered around the reasons behind an invitation—the reasons we rarely consider because they seem so inherently obvious.

Foremost, the purpose of any invitation is to ask someone to an event that you are planning. The fact that someone is planning an event naturally implies preparation. When you prepare for such a celebration, you choose how you will celebrate it, from the food to the flowers, the music to the main course. With weddings, we all know how much planning—and money—can go into even the tiniest of details.

You have to decide if you want it simple, maybe with only cake and punch, or more elaborate, possible with a reception and casual buffet, or if you want a formal, sit-down, multi-course dinner. You not only have to decide what you will serve to eat but what beverages will accompany your food. Many couples decide to include alcohol as part of their celebration, which not only increases the expense but also requires extra servers, bartenders, bar stations, glassware, and the alcoholic libations themselves.

That day when I sat down in my study and began reading through the various nuptial invitations that arrived that day, my mind began reeling with the implications of how all this applied to the wedding at Cana—the occasion for Jesus' first public miracle.

Invitation to a Wedding

I must confess that I've always been intrigued, even troubled at times, about why our Lord's first display of His almighty, instantaneous power was at a social event in which very few people knew what He did. And the fact that what He did was turn gallons of water into the most delicious, flavorful wine— stunning, yes, but worthy of His attention, let alone His power?

It just doesn't make sense. Forgive me, but at times I still think he could have chosen a better place and did something far more spectacular than just turning water into wine. There were plenty of other miracles He did that I, in my humanity, would have chosen to do before what might seem to be merely a party trick.

Think about it. We're talking about the Almighty God in the flesh. This is the same God who created matter with His speech. He set the stars in the sky. He created the planet with all its diverse forms of life. He opened up the Red Sea and sent plague after plague upon Egypt to deliver his children. Later, as He walked the planet, He fed five thousand people and more. He raised Lazarus from the dead, touched the bier of a dead child to turn a funeral into a party, healed a woman who had been bleeding for years, and raised Himself from the dead.

This was the same Jesus who walked on the water and calmed a storm with only a few words. The same Jesus that conquered sin, hell, and death. The same Jesus who was transfigured in front of Peter, James, and John, and had Moses and Elijah stand next to Him and converse while God confirmed Him. This was the same Jesus who healed the man with a withered hand. The same Jesus who healed the lame man at the pool of Bethesda. This was the same Jesus who spat on the ground and used the mud to heal a blind man.

If there was anything I would have done as my first public miracle, it would have been something irrevocably supernatural in nature—something that would have *made* people believe that I was the Messiah. Jesus could have done anything He wanted but, as we see in this passage, chose to turn water into wine.

Jesus could have done anything He wanted but, as we see in this passage, chose to turn water into wine.

On the third day a wedding took place at Cana in Galilee. Jesus' mother was there, and Jesus and His disciples had also been invited to the wedding. When the wine was gone, Jesus' mother said to Him, "They have no more wine."

"Woman, why do you involve me?" Jesus replied. "My hour has not yet come."

His mother said to the servants, "Do whatever He tells you."

Nearby stood six stone water jars, the kind used by the Jews for ceremonial washing, each holding from twenty to thirty gallons.

Jesus said to the servants, "Fill the jars with water"; so they filled them to the brim.

Then He told them, "Now draw some out and take it to the master of the banquet."

They did so, and the master of the banquet tasted the water that had been turned into wine. He did not realize where it had come from, though the servants who had drawn the water knew. Then He called the bridegroom aside and said, "Everyone brings out the choice wine first and then the cheaper wine after the guests have had too much to drink; but you have saved the best till now." (John 2:1–10)

Invisible Troubles

When it comes to us understanding what was happening at the wedding at Cana, and perhaps why Jesus chose it to perform the miracle we have recorded as His first, then we need to know the importance of a wedding during this period. In the West, weddings of today are based almost entirely on the feelings that people have for one another. A couple dates for a while, falls in love, and decides to spend the rest of their lives together. Then they go about planning their wedding.

In ancient Eastern cultures, however, marriages were often arranged and based on something more than just the love between two people. Weddings united houses of families and, in the case of royalty or the wealthy, brought about more power and allies. Therefore, a wedding in Jewish antiquity brought with it far-reaching ramifications.

A large wedding party, then as now, was directly proportional to the level of planning and resources that went into pulling it off. Therefore, the fact that Jesus, Mary, His mother, and His disciples attended implies that this wasn't just a small ceremony with a few close friends and family. In fact, there were apparently so many guests and so many details involved that the families hired someone to manage the feast. The Bible does not tell us about the bride and groom, but we can infer that their families had wealth, some level of power, and enough notoriety that would cause Jesus to want to attend the party.

The bridegroom and bride declared their vows and said their "I do's." Everyone then headed to the wedding feast. The food was delightful, and people continued to dine. The laughter was boisterous, and everyone was in high spirits. But what *can* go wrong often *does* go wrong. While everyone was enjoying themselves, Mary and her perceptive eye picked up on a problem that many others did not see. The hosts were running out of wine.

For a party this lavish and a family this well off, it would have been a social embarrassment they couldn't live down if the secret had gotten out that they were in short supply of anything. Mary then calls Jesus' attention to the fact that the family—horror of horrors—had run out of wine. The wedding feast was in peril, and the groom and family were just minutes away from being humiliated. This family was in desperate need of assistance.

While it may not seem like a matter of life and death to us today, this family's name and honor were on the line. Their identity was at stake. I would imagine that the patriarchs of either family had worked decades to gain the honor that was associated with their names. To have all of that come crashing down by a small oversight would have been an unimaginable embarrassment. Even worse, according to Scripture, the only people aware of the problem were Mary, Jesus, and the servants at the wedding feast.

Seeing that no one in the wedding family was aware of the problem, they weren't aware of the solution in their presence. I cannot pass up the opportunity to direct your attention to the problems you didn't even know you had and the many ways God has blessed you when you didn't even know it. If God told you everything He did for you, everything He kept you from, and everything He kept from you, you would sprint to the altar at the nearest church and begin repenting of all your doubt, fear, disbelief, distrust, and anxiety. When I look back over my own life and consider what could have happened, how I could have been hurt, how I could have lost my life, and where I could be right now, I am brought to the brink of tears.

There are times when you have to stand back and praise the Master for saving you from what could have happened and who and what you could have been. You cannot afford to miss this point. Very few individuals in a party of what could have been hundreds knew about the depletion of the wine. So few knew that even the supervisor of the feast and the family were in complete ignorance. This was even after Jesus performed the miracle.

The Vintner's work in our lives addresses issues we didn't even know we had, and thankfully, He addresses some of our issues in secret. Maybe you used to be the most cantankerous people on the planet, but you've noticed that He has softened your heart. Or perhaps you were once ruled by fear, but you can't even track how and when the Lord removed it from your heart. One day it was present; the next day, it was gone. You might have been beating yourselves up for years with self-condemnation, but the Master stepped in and imputed unto you a righteousness you know didn't come from you, and you've been the freest you have ever been in your life.

*The Vintner's work in our lives addresses issues
we didn't even know we had, and thankfully, He
addresses some of our issues in secret.*

Thank God for taking care of our invisible trouble.

This miracle at the wedding had to be done in secret to keep dishonor from hitting the bridegroom and his family. Therefore, what Jesus did was change someone's dishonor to praise and honor. Too often, our crushing and fermentation seem so painful to us, but we don't realize that the agony we run from the most is the instrument the Vintner uses to press and strain out of us what we don't need so that only what we do need will remain.

In essence, we flee from something temporary at the expense of the eternal because we're focusing on the ugliness of today instead of the beauty of what God has promised us tomorrow. "For our light and momentary troubles are achieving for us an eternal glory that far outweighs them all. So we fix our eyes not on what is seen, but on what is unseen, since what is seen is temporary, but what is unseen is eternal" (2 Cor. 4:17–18).

Wine, Not Whine

I love the way Mary went into action when she discovered the fact that the family was out of wine. Like any good mother, any gracious guest, she immediately turns her attention to the most expedient way of solving the problem and averting disaster. She goes to her Son and relays the situation to Him as if he—the Almighty God incarnate—wasn't already aware.

And at first, you might think Jesus' response, "This isn't my time," was disrespectful. It sort of has that "Not now, Mom!" sense that we've all heard children, no matter their age, use in response to a parent's urgent request. Considering the fact that Mary was fully aware of who Jesus was and possessed at least a slim understanding of His capabilities, we can appreciate how the Master is intimately aware of every conundrum that we would ever face.

So why Mary would think her intervention was necessary when she had to have known that Jesus was already on top of things? Consider the fact that Mary rose from her seat, ventured to the servants at the feast, and vehemently instructed them with the words, "Whatever He tells you to do, do it!" This alerts us to the fact that Jesus had to have performed other supernatural feats with Mary as a witness, therefore putting her in the position of having full confidence in Jesus' identity and power as God. But something quite human comes on the heels of that observation. Mary feels compelled to do something—to go to Jesus and *make* Him solve the problem. If there was no wine, then someone had to whine.

Have you noticed how we have the tendency to rush the Lord when we discover a problem in our lives? We think, from our limited understanding of the quandary, that we must tell God what's happening. We arrogantly presume that he's either not involved with the situation and hasn't already provided an answer, or that He didn't allow the problem to manifest and that life had somehow managed to sneak something by Him. But if we really believe that God is God, why in the world would we think that we could inform Him of anything?

When we place Mary's actions in the light and perspective of the Husbandman and the grapes He grows, we get a much better understanding of her presumption. It's not that Mary believed Jesus couldn't replenish the wine. The problem was that she presumed to have a better understanding of what was happening than Jesus did. It's the equivalent of a grape saying to the Husbandman, "Excuse me, but now is the right time for you to act. Now is the time for you to transform me!" How could the grape possibly know? Who is the One who has been cultivating vines and growing grapes for eons before this particular berry began hanging from the branch?

Therein is our problem.

God has designed, equipped, and called each of us to accomplish many great things. He has given us a vision, promising that He would bring it to pass. Why then are we so prone to lose sight of the fact that the Master is the one who gave us the idea and not the other way around? Probably more than anything else, the one message I have to tell people that I mentor and counsel over and over and over again is that God's timing is flawless. His clock is perfect.

God has designed, equipped, and called each of us to accomplish many great things. He has given us a vision, promising that He would bring it to pass.

Over and over again, I have to thank God for sticking with his timetable for my life and not bending to my will. I can look back over my life and see where God could have answered me right then with what I thought I wanted and allow it to destroy me.

With the utmost gratitude, I salute Him for keeping from me what I considered the best thing for me at the time.

If you're anything like me, you realize the folly of begging God for something, and when He gives it to you, you murmur and complain about what you got. We have the craziest habit of wanting what we want until we get it. Whereas, if we waited for the fullness of God's timing to come to pass, we would see that His ordained season carries within it an unforeseen amount of grace and protection.

When Jesus responded to Mary about why she was so concerned, our True Vine made it clear He already had the situation covered under control. Even though Mary pressed the issue with the servants, Jesus was wise enough to turn her premature actions into something He used to His advantage, which raises other questions: *If Jesus is God, he had to have seen this coming? And if He saw it coming, doesn't that mean He planned to be there and perform a miracle?*

We must remember that our God sees the end from the beginning. There is no problem for which He doesn't already have a solution. Therefore, I wholeheartedly believe that Jesus *knew* what was going to happen at the wedding at Cana, and this is precisely why Mary shouldn't have been up in arms in the first place.

We must remember that our God sees the end from the beginning.

Everything God does is strategic. Never do we witness God making a mistake or running late for His divine appointments with us. Though I might be taken by surprise with the situations that befall me in life, there has never been a moment when I ran to God with the words, "Lord, I didn't even see this coming," and He responded, "I didn't either!"

Consequently, consider this conclusion: Jesus, our God in physical form, planned for the wedding. Remember, our Master will use *anything* to point us back to our need for Him, even our mistakes and things we didn't see coming. If Jesus can plan for and use the lack of wine at a wedding feast for His glory while staving off the family's public embarrassment and shame, I cannot help but believe that He will use the smallest details of my life to propel His Kingdom plan and me forward!

Instantly Extraordinary

Throughout this entire book, we've been discussing how the Lord develops and transforms us. Across these pages, you've repeatedly read the word *process*. This word, in and of itself, denotes the passage of time. For the most part, transformation isn't an event, and it's definitely not something that happens only once. As I continue to grow in my relationship with the Lord, I am appreciating the fact that He takes His time with me. He doesn't rush with any of us because anything valuable is also something worth waiting for. After all, excellence is not produced in haste.

But there are occasions when it seems like there is no time for process—those moments when something must be done *now*. There is no waiting. There are no seasons. There comes a time in your life when you need a word, a solution, or a miracle now. When dying on the operating table, you don't need someone to run you through the process of the entire surgery. The surgeon should have started working the day before!

We see this with the woman with the issue of blood. The woman was already dying, and we infer that it was her desperation for healing that drove her to press through the crowd and touch the hem of Jesus' garment. Or what of the woman who was bent and bowed over for eighteen years (Luke 13:12)? Was it better for the Lord to tell her about what He would do to heal her or say, "Woman, thou art loosed"?

What I am trying to get you to see is that, though the Lord develops us through a process that transforms us, He is fully aware of those moments when a season of change will take too long. There are times in our lives when He instantly brings forth in us what is necessary at that moment. Those are the instances when He moves from working on us through process to making us immediately incredible.

Prompted by Mary's concern, Jesus takes advantage of what was about to be a serious party pooper. Rather than the shame of telling guests there was no more wine, crisis was not only averted but changed into an opportunity for divine wine. For in just a matter of moments, the water that was ordinary was changed into something extraordinary, and that is precisely what the entire process is all about.

The best that we could bring to the Master is our ordinary, customary, dime-a-dozen selves. Without the intervention of the Vintner, we are left water that is common all over the world. Therefore, our worth is not found in what we are in and of ourselves, but in what the Vintner does with us. This is why we must learn to divorce our value from what we produce and link it to the finished work of Christ being crushed on the cross and whatever else He chooses to do in our lives.

---

*The best that we could bring to the Master is our
ordinary, customary, dime-a-dozen selves.*

The moment we decide otherwise, our crushing is,
indeed, the end. As a result, the pain we feel when we
lost the original harvest that we produced is what naturally follows our misunderstanding that our wine is
not our works, but God's. So how could the crushing
He begins in our lives be the end-all-be-all of who
and what we are? No! Surely, there is more.

After the servants filled the pots—*without the
knowledge of anyone else at the feast*—Jesus tells the servants to draw out a sampling of the water and take it
to the manager of the feast. Oddly enough, upon the
supervisor tasting what was once water, He realizes
that He sampled the best wine He has ever tasted.

Notice, too, that no one, not even the servants,
knew *when* the water was transformed to wine. All
they knew was that, right before their very eyes and
without their knowledge, a final product had been
presented. As it is with the Lord working out our
issues in secret, the Lord transformed the water to
wine in secret by hurrying the process along so that
the family's honor might be saved.

Similarly, some of us can point back to moments

in our lives when the Master either dealt away with the process altogether or sped it up to save us from what was most certainly about to befall us. I don't know about you, but it's here that I am going to take a moment and offer praise to the One who is sensitive about the times and seasons in my life while being completely aware of when it's necessary to make me instantly extraordinary.

The Best for Last

During the process of our crushing, fermentation, and transformation into God's wine, we often lose sight of what our Master is doing and become consumed with impatience. "When, Lord?" we ask. "When will I see what you're up to? When will my pain stop? When will my life turn around? When will my loss subside? When will I experience your joy and peace? *When, Lord, when?*"

Perhaps you're asking that question right now. You've sensed that the Vintner has been doing a mighty work in your life and that He has bottled you for distribution or is ready to pour you out for all the world to taste. However, there seems to be a delay, and you're questioning Him about when He will do what He said He was going to do. You see others experiencing and walking in their promise while wondering when your day will come.

The supervisor of the feast mentioned the tradition of how wine was served (John 2:10). Normally, the best would be served first and, once the guests have had their fill and spirits were high, the cheaper wine would be served last. This is *man's* order. He always wants to put his best foot forward right at the beginning, and I do see the value in doing so. After all, you only get one shot to make a great first impression. However, when it comes to His transformation of us from water into wine and how the Master does things in the Kingdom, we see that He takes a different approach. Again, He allows man to come to the end of Himself so that He could have His way.

God always saves the best for last!

God always saves the best for last!

Do you realize that what took some people fifteen or even twenty years to accomplish, God can bring about for you in less than a day? So when it comes to the question of "when?" that burns in your heart, remember the same Husbandman who matured and cultivated you in your vine and grape stages is the same Vintner who crushed, fermented, and bottled you in your wine stages.

God is fully aware of your times and seasons. You needn't worry about anything, save keeping your eyes on the Master who has already called over the servants who will present what you have to the supervisor of the feast. The party is in full swing. The guests are present. Man's temporary and less-desirable wine is running out. Your time is almost here. Remain patient. Your water is about to be drawn out to be sampled and served.

Crushing is never the end.

Your best is yet to come!

CHAPTER 15

New Wine

*Dear friends, now we are children of God, and
what we will be has not yet been made known.
But we know that when Christ appears, we shall
be like Him, for we shall see Him as He is.*

—1 John 3:2

As we conclude our time together, I pray that you
have come to believe, like I have, that our crushing is not the end. Our losses only lead to enlightening.
Death is not the end. Like a seed that dies in the ground,
our crushing sprouts into something more beautiful and
productive. Pairing that concept with the fact that our
God works in seasonal cycles, we are left with the outcome that we were never meant to exist only in one form.

I would go as far as saying that we were never meant to die but to continuously grow even better with every stage. Even the cells of our bodies testify to the truth of this point, for our bodies are programmed to repair themselves. If we are cut, instantly red blood cells work to clot the injury and set about stitching the skin and fighting infection.

We are meant to live.

This vineyard in which the Husbandman has planted us isn't something He has created in order to engage in a hobby and fill His time. Everything the Master does is for a distinct purpose. *We* are the ones who fail to recognize this. And, if you're like me, you've noticed the fact that God is uniquely persistent in His desire to complete this process within us. His love drives Him to chase after us in the hope that we will open ourselves up to His plan, His way, and His transformation process in our lives. He never gives up on us, and He never abandons us when we've decided to go astray and handle things our own way. He simply allows us to come to the end of ourselves.

Everything the Master does is for a distinct purpose.

We see this when Jeremiah is sent down to the potter's house to watch him work with clay on the wheel. The potter molds the clay as he sees fit, shaping it for whatever purpose he so desires. Something goes wrong, however. For some reason, the clay becomes misshapen. The problem wasn't with the potter, though, but with the clay, for our potter's methods are perfect. Notice, then, what the potter does. He doesn't throw away the clay. No, the potter merely starts over, reworking and molding the clay into whatever form he desires.

Similarly, the Master desires to do the same with us, and we see Him making this statement even with wine. All we need for proof of this is His Word, and it comes through with undeniable truth.

> I will sing for the one I love a song about His vineyard:
>> My loved one had a vineyard on a fertile hillside.
>> He dug it up and cleared it of stones and planted it with the choicest vines.
>> He built a watchtower in it and cut out a winepress as well.
>> Then He looked for a crop of good grapes, but it yielded only bad fruit. (Isa. 5:1–2)

Isaiah paints an excellent portrait of what the Master sought to do with humanity, even from the very beginning in the Garden of Eden. However, like the clay, something went wrong. God didn't create a race of robots, but one of individuals who could think for themselves. He chose to create us this way in the hopes that we would choose to love Him like He chose to love us. For a fruitful relationship is one in which its constituents have chosen to participate. If one forced their will on the other, it's no longer a relationship but a rape.

Upon reading the rest of the allegory of the Vintner and His vineyard in the fifth chapter of Isaiah, we see judgment being pronounced on those He planted in the choicest of places. But we mustn't stop there. If we consider the rest of Isaiah, we see God revealing the plan He has to redeem not only Israel but also the whole of humanity.

This plan was not just for us to be saved from the punishment of our sins. It couldn't have been. For the Lord to address the actions but not address the heart is for Him to set Himself up for another failed vineyard and crop that would have borne Him nothing but compounded grief and heartache.

Instead, the Master Vintner becomes a part of the vineyard. He plants Himself as the True Vine from which we would grow. By this, God changed our very nature so that not only would He completely vanquish the sin, but He would also take us further and deal with our hearts in our crushing and fermentation.

The Master Vintner becomes a part of the vineyard.

Putting this in perspective with Christ's actions, would it have made sense for Jesus to die on the cross but not rise again? Similarly, how could we ever think the Lord would plant us only to kill us and let us die? No! There must be more.

The wedding at Cana wasn't a one-off instance in which the Lord would showcase His power. He could have chosen something far more fantastic to grab the attention of everyone there. After all, looking back at the entire ordeal, only a few individuals even knew what he did. The wedding at Cana was a symbol of the wine-making process through which the Lord would take us because He wasn't satisfied with merely saving us.

God loves us, and love necessitates the desire to be near the focus of that love. Therefore, how could our crushing be the end of our lives when our eternal Lord has telegraphed His hope to be with us eternally? The Lord hasn't sought to destroy us—he looks to remake us, remold us, and reshape us into something that looks just like Him.

You may have just come out of the most harrowing experience of your life. You've endured a crushing like no other, and you're beginning to see that the Master isn't done with you. Your pain was just the beginning, and it's starting to dawn on you that maybe—just maybe—the Husbandman and Vintner of souls has something excellent in store for you.

Or perhaps you're reading the final pages of this book while you're still suffering under the crushing foot of the Master. You've lost everything and the glimmer of life that decorated your eyes is dying. You're disoriented and can't find your way to get out of bed in the morning, let alone become holy wine in the hands of the Lord.

But no matter where you are, my friend, do not give up! You must hold on. Where you are is not the destination of your life. God would not have engaged in so much work on you and in you to abandon you. On the contrary, He has invested much in you because of your value and what He sees in you. His eye rests on something in your future that your current pain is blinding you from seeing.

And *when*—not *if*—you have come through this crushing and fermentation, having been renewed and transformed, your life will be the peculiar new vintage that comes only from the heavenly casks of the

Master. You'll be a wine that the entire world hopes not only to sample, but also to emulate.

Can you see it now? You're a sign that points others to the God who transformed you. Your pain, suffering, metamorphosis, and transformation is a temporary moment that will produce the private reserve for which everyone will clamor. And the instant in which others sip from the goblet you have offered, your bouquet will point directly back to the Vintner with whom you share a supernaturally matrimonial connection, causing them to ask not only what they must do to be saved, but also about the process you endured to become the choicest of wines of which the world has ever partaken.

You're a sign that points others to the God who transformed you.

Never allow the lying words of the enemy to take root and poison the wine God wants to produce in your life. In those moments, when everything falls apart, when you don't know how you can go on or even if you will go on, please remember this message from my heart.

Your crushing is not the end!
It's only the beginning.

About the Author

T. D. Jakes is a #1 *New York Times* bestselling author of more than forty books and the CEO of TDJ Enterprises, LLP. He is the founder of the thirty-thousand-member Potter's House Church, and his television ministry program, *The Potter's Touch*, is watched by 3.3 million viewers every week. He has produced Grammy Award–winning music and such films as *Heaven Is for Real*, *Sparkle*, and *Jumping the Broom*. A master communicator, he hosts MegaFest, Woman Thou Art Loosed, and other conferences attended by tens of thousands. T. D. Jakes lives in Dallas with his wife and five children. Visit www.tdjakes.com.